Street by Street

CHES

BUCKLEY, CONN... QUAY,
FLINT, MOLD

Blacon, Broughton, Christleton, Ewloe, Hawarden, Mickle Trafford, Mynydd Isa, Northop, Queensferry, Saltney, Saughall, Shotton, Soughton, Waverton

C000091440

2nd edition November 2004
© Automobile Association Developments
Limited 2004

Original edition printed May 2001

Ordnance Survey® This product includes map data
licensed from Ordnance Survey ®
with the permission of the Controller of Her Majesty's
Stationery Office. © Crown copyright 2004.
All rights reserved. Licence number 399221.

Published by AA Publishing (a trading name of
Automobile Association Developments Limited, whose
registered office is Southwood East, Apollo Rise,
Farnborough, Hampshire, GU14 0JW. Registered
number 1878835).

Mapping produced by the Cartography Department of
The Automobile Association. (A02238)

A CIP Catalogue record for this book is available from
the British Library.

Printed by GRAFIASA S.A., Porto, Portugal

Ref: ML081z

Key to map pages	ii-iii
Key to map symbols	iv–1
Enlarged map pages	2-3
Main map pages	4-51
Index – towns & villages	52
Index – streets	52-57
Index – featured places	58
Acknowledgements	58

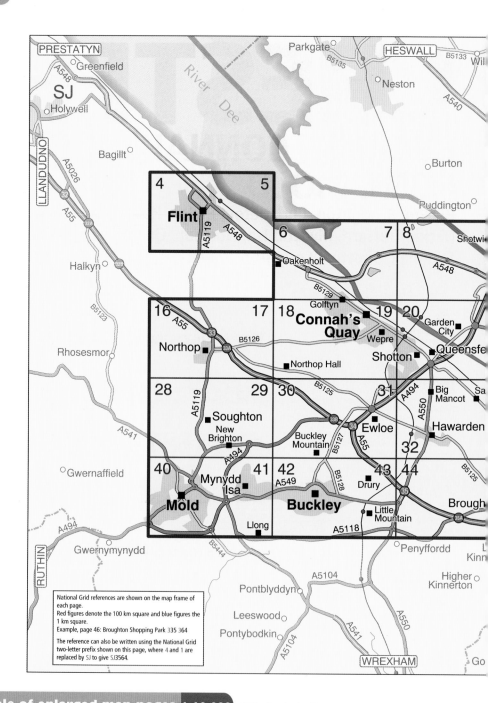

PRESTATYN

Greenfield

SJ

Holywell

Bagillt

River Dee

Parkgate

HESWALL

B5133

Wil

Neston

A540

Burton

Puddington

| 4 | 5 |

Flint

A5119

A548

| 6 | | 7 | 8 |

Oakenholt

Shotwi

A548

B5129

Halkyn

Golftyn

| 16 | 17 | 18 | | 19 | 20 |

A55

Connah's Quay

Garden City

B5126

Queensfe

Northop

Wepre

Rhosesmor

Northop Hall

Shotton

B5125

| 28 | 29 | 30 | | 31 | | Big Mancot | Sa |

A5119

A494

A550

Soughton

New Brighton

Buckley Mountain

Ewloe

Hawarden

A541

A494

B5127

A55

| 32 |

B5125

Gwernaffield

| 40 | 41 | 42 | | 43 | 44 |

Mynydd Isa

A549

B5128

Drury

Mold

Buckley

Little Mountain

Brough

Llong

A5118

B5444

Gwernymynydd

Penyffordd

Kinn

RUTHIN

LLANDUDNO

A5104

Higher Kinnerton

Pontblyddyn

Leeswood

A550

Pontybodkin

A5104

A541

WREXHAM

Go

A548

A5026

A55

National Grid references are shown on the map frame of each page.
Red figures denote the 100 km square and blue figures the 1 km square.
Example, page 46: Broughton Shopping Park 335 364

The reference can also be written using the National Grid two-letter prefix shown on this page, where 4 and 1 are replaced by SJ to give SJ3564.

Scale of enlarged map pages 1:10,000   6.3 inches to 1 mile

0   1/4   miles   1/2

0   1/4   1/2   kilometres   3/4   1

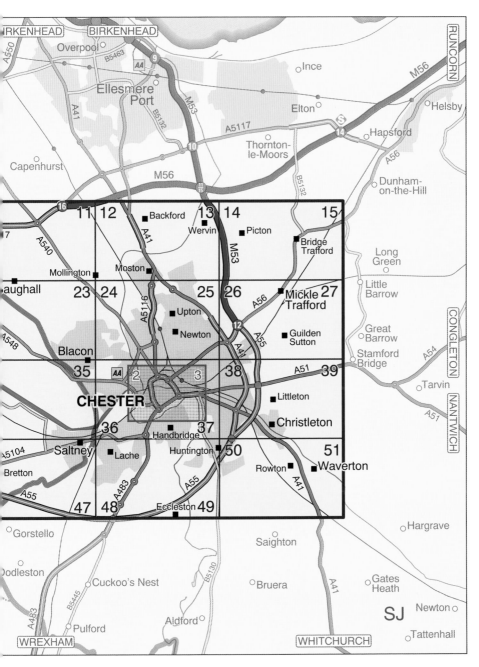

iv

Junction 9	Motorway & junction	⊖	Underground station
Services	Motorway service area	——⊖——	Light railway & station
	Primary road single/dual carriageway	+++++++++	Preserved private railway
Services	Primary road service area	LC	Level crossing
	A road single/dual carriageway	•—•—•—•	Tramway
	B road single/dual carriageway	-----------	Ferry route
	Other road single/dual carriageway	....	Airport runway
	Minor/private road, access may be restricted	— · — · — · —	County, administrative boundary
← ←	One-way street	▼▼▼▼▼▼▼▼▼▼	Mounds
	Pedestrian area	**17**	Page continuation 1:15,000
============	Track or footpath	**3**	Page continuation to enlarged scale 1:10,000
▮▮▮▮▮▮▮▮ ▮▮▮▮▮▮▮▮	Road under construction		River/canal, lake
[⌐ = = = ¬]	Road tunnel		Aqueduct, lock, weir
AA	AA Service Centre	465 ▲ Winter Hill	Peak (with height in metres)
P	Parking		Beach
P+🚌	Park & Ride		Woodland
🚌	Bus/coach station		Park
⇌	Railway & main railway station	✝ ✝ ✝ ✝	Cemetery
⇌	Railway & minor railway station		Built-up area

Featured building		Abbey, cathedral or priory	
City wall		Castle	
Hospital with 24-hour A&E department		Historic house or building	
Post Office		National Trust property	Wakehurst Place NT
Public library		Museum or art gallery	
Tourist Information Centre		Roman antiquity	
Seasonal Tourist Information Centre		Ancient site, battlefield or monument	
Petrol station, 24-hour — Major suppliers only		Industrial interest	
Church/chapel		Garden	
Public toilets		Garden Centre — Garden Centre Association Member	
Toilet with disabled facilities		Garden Centre — Wyevale Garden Centre	
Public house — AA recommended		Farm or animal centre	
Restaurant — AA inspected		Zoological or wildlife collection	
Hotel — AA inspected	Madeira Hotel	Bird collection	
Theatre or performing arts centre		Nature reserve	
Cinema		Aquarium	
Golf course		Visitor or heritage centre	
Camping — AA inspected		Country park	
Caravan site — AA inspected		Cave	
Camping & caravan site — AA inspected		Windmill	
Theme park		Distillery, brewery or vineyard	

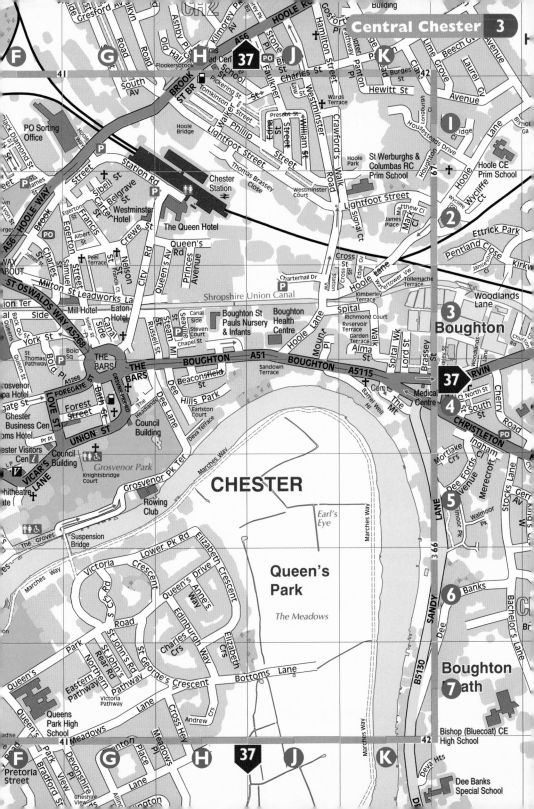

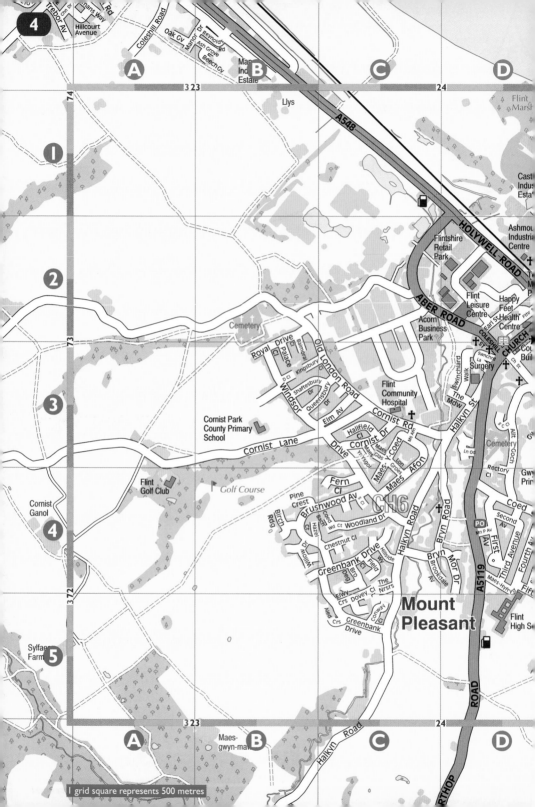

E F G H

25 26 74

I

2

73

3

Dyke St

Flint FC

Marsh Lane

Castle Road
Roskell

Henry Taylor St

FLINT

CHESTER ROAD

Borough Gv

Trelawny Av

Ysgol Croes Atti Primary School

Avenue

Maes
Dre

Kings Av

Maes Gwyn

Woodfield Avenue

Queens Av

Wales

Cae Hir

Maes Alaw

Avenue

PO

Ffordd Llewelyn

Cae
Derw

Albert Av

Bryn

Siriol

Julius Close

Caesar Av

Deva Cl

Mill Croft

Englefield Drive

Aris Cft

St Marys RC Primary School

Croes Atti La

CHESTER

LC

Glan
Gors

Garth Canol

St Richard Gwyn RC High School

Rhos

Moel Parc

Aber Las

Balin

Bryn

4

6

372

5

Coed Onn Road

ROAD

A548

Leadbrook Drive

Onnen

Gwyn

Bryn

Cwm
Eithion

Fran Swr

Cae
Bychan

Ffordd y

Min
Awel

Hwyfden

25 26

E F G H

Leadbrook Drive

lg paper
Mill Lane

Paper

Oakenholt

6

A B C D

3 27 28

I

5 72

2

A548

3 Oakenholt

Old Paper Mill Lane

Paper Mill Lane

CHESTER RD

Kelsterton Road

White Sands

71

4

Oakenholt Lane

5

3 70

Cheshire Farm

Deeside College

KELSTERTON ROAD

B5129

Deeside Stadium

Connahs Quay Sports Centre

Kelsterton

Connahs Quay High School

Golftyn Lane

College

3 27 28

A B C D

Top-y-fron

18

Hafod

Courser Drive

I grid square represents 500 metres

E   F   G   H

29   30

I

WEIGHBR

Weighbridge   Road

2

Works

Weighbridge

Road

3

8

71

4

North Road

Ring Road

Coatings By Pass Rd

Steel Works

Two

Coatings

River

Road

5

Golftyn

70

30

FET

PO

Bank Road

Dee Vw Rd

Wr Brook

Dunbar Cl

Talfryn Av

Queen's Cl

Kent Cl

Kings Road

Nant Road

Union St

New
Pl

Cem Rd

Osbourne Ct

CHURCH ST   CHURCH HILL

Surg

Quay La

DOCK

Cable St

E   F   19   G   H

Road

Fishermans Rd

Dock Rd

Garthorpe Av

Derwen Close

Owyan Cl

Cemetery

CP

HIGH

Tuscan

River D

8

A   B   C   D

331   32

1

WEIGHBRIDGE   ROAD

A548

Weighbridge   Road

2

Works

Tenth   Av

Tenth Avenue

3

7

Parkway

4

Fourth

Pa
Bu
Ce

Sixth Av

5

Par

370   331   32

A   B   20   C   D

1 grid square represents 500 metres

Shotwick

Shotwick Dale

Cheshire County
Flintshire

Shotwick Lane

Woodbank Lane

Green La (West)

WELSH

A550

A51

A548

Second Av

Parkway

First Avenue

Drive A

Drive B

Drive C

First Avenue

Drive D

DROME RD
B5441

WELSH ROAD

Green Lane

East

Deeside Industrial Estate

Deva Business Park

Old Marsh Farm

CK ROAD

E F G H

I

2

3

10

4

5

21

33 34

72

71

370

Woodbank

10

A   B   C   D

335   36

WELSH ROAD

Shotwick Dale

Woodbank Lane

A550

1

72

New Covert

2

Woodbank Lane

A5117

A540

G

Council Building

Shotwicklodge Farm

3

9

71

Castle Farm

Green Farm

4

Parkgate House

Lodge

Thomas Wedge Junior School

PO

Park Way

Church Road

5

Shotwick House

Darlington

Smithy

Anvil

Surgery

370

335   36

A   B   **22**   C   D

Surgery

Vernon Ct

Chapel Ct

e Wy

Fox Lea

Meadows La

Crofter's Wy

Hermitage Ct

anhill

Road

Hermit

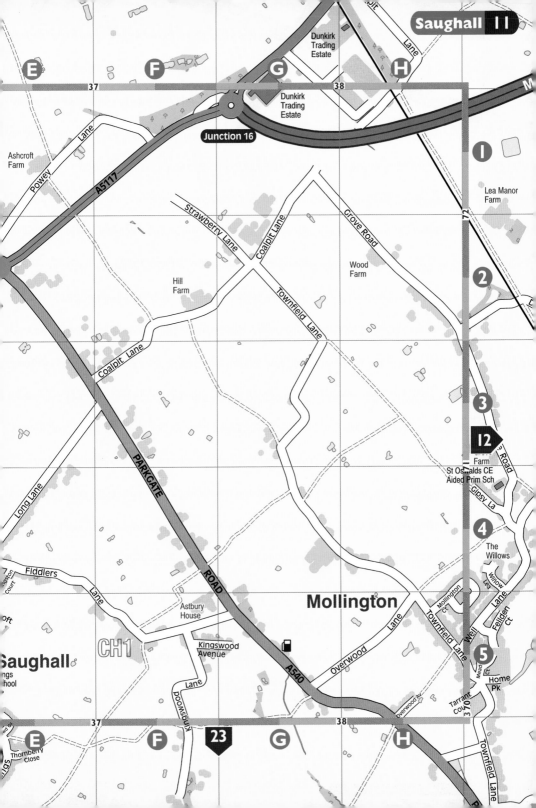

14

Ashwood
House   **A**   **B**   **C**   **D**

3 43   44

Ashwood Lane

I

72

CH2

Werv..

2

Picton Lane

Mill Brook

Picton

Green Lane

3

13

Ash Hay Lane

Wervin Road

4

Fox

M53

Ash
Hey

Covert

5

Lane

Ash Hay Lane

Picton Lane

3 70

A   **B**   **26**   **C**   **D**

3 43   44

Lane   Fox

Covert

Picto.
Gorse

Salter's

Lane

Cemete..

**Mickle
Trafford**

..ngfields

Vil
Sc..

..hool

I grid square represents 500 metres

Moss House

Hob Lane

Manor Farm

mbolds fford

INCE LANE

E F G H

45 46

I

Cornhill Farm

72 A56

Park Farm

INCE LANE B5132

2

WAR

Morley Bridge

B5132

WARRINGTON ROAD

A56

71

3

Hassals Lane

Bridge Trafford

Morley Hall

4

WARRINGTON ROAD

Wildmoor La

B5170

5

Plemstall

treet

ee Road

Glebe Mdw

Linden

Plemstall Wy

Plemstall Lane

27

Holly Close

Stile End

Plemstall

E F G H

45 46

Morley

Wayside Court

Holme Farm

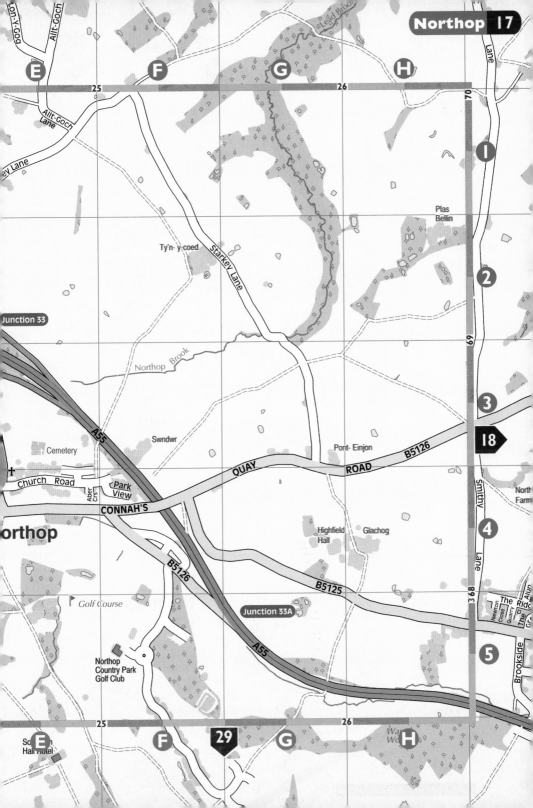

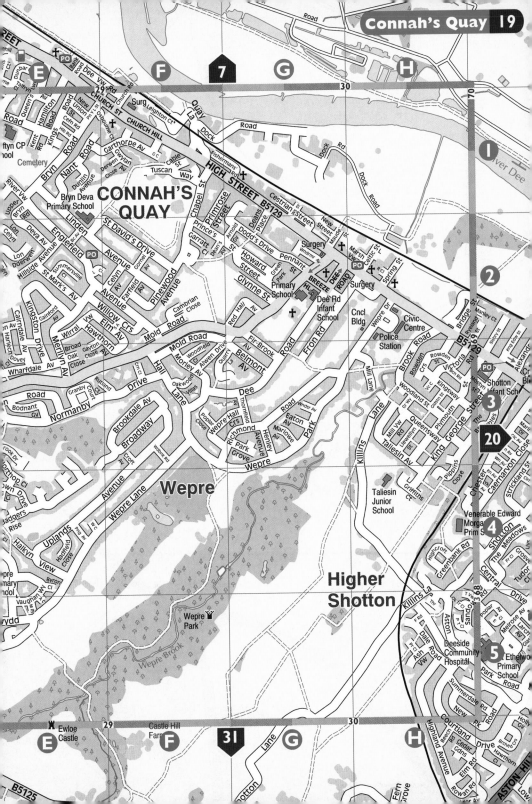

E F **9** G H

Deeside
Industrial
Estate

33 34 **70**

Deva
Business
Park

I

Old Marsh
Farm

A550

Garden City
Industrial Estate

B5441

Deva
Business
Park

Hawthorn Vw

Cedar Av

2

Willow
Farm

Sealand Child
Health Centre

Sandy La

Queen's Rd

Dee Rd

The Gateway
To Wales Hotel

69

A548 SEALAND ROAD

PO

B5441

Riverside Pk

Villa Rd

3

A494

Fox's Drive

Road

Owl Halt
Industrial Estate

22

Manor

Meadow Vw

North Gn

Ferry Cl

South Gn

East Gn

Sealand Manor

4

Deva
Industrial Park

68

Deva
Industrial
Park

5

Factory

Rectors La

Road

Babbage Road

Factory

Alvis Rd

Deva
Ho

Sandycroft
Industrial Estate

Church

33 E F **33** St Ives Wy G H River Dee

CHESTER

Sandycroft
Industrial Est

St Ives Wy

34

Glendale Av

Prince Will

ancot

Plemstall

I5

E   F   G   H

I

2

69

3

70

Holme Farm

LC

The Hall

Longster Trail

ilden
tton

Lane

Old   Hall
Park

Hillton
Rd

The
Vetches

Cinder
Lane

Cinder Lane

klands

Church Lane

Station Lane

Wicker Lane

The Byatts

4

BARROW

B5132

5

River   Gowy

**Stamford
Bridge**

WARRI

Street
ee Road

Plemstall WV

Plemstall

St Peter's Way

Glebe
MdW

Holly
Close

Morley

Thomas Cl

Wayside
Court

Stile
End

No Cl

45   46

E   F   **39**   G   H

45   46

Golf Course

Vicars Cross

TARVIN ROAD

A5

34

Deeside House

A

B

22

C

Birchenfields Farm

D

3 35

36

River Dee

1

Sealand Nursery

Deeside Lane

67

2

3

Beeches Farm

33

B5129

River Dee

Cop House Farm

99

4

5

Hawarden Airport

3 65

3 35

36

A

B

46

C

D

Broughton Industrial Estate

Well House Farm

Broughton

1 grid square represents 500 metres

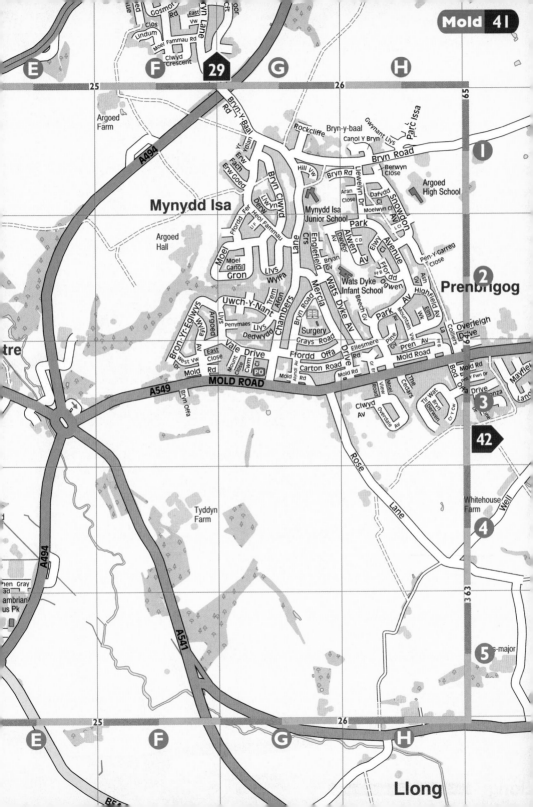

E F 29 G H

25 26 65

Gosmot
Rd
East
Vw
Clos
Lindum
Moel Fammau Rd
Clwyd Crescent

I

Bryn-y-Baal Rd

Argoed Farm

A494

Rockcliffe
Bryn-y-baal
Canol Y Bryn
Gwynant Llys
Parc Issa
Bryn Road
Berwyn Close

Mynydd Isa

Hill Vw
Bryn Rd
Bryn Clwyd
Llwyn
Derw
Ffordd Fer
Heol Fammau
Mynydd Isa Junior School
Aran Close
Dafydd Cl
Moelwyn Cl
Llewelyn Dr
Snowdon Av
Argoed High School

Argoed Hall

Moel Ganol
Moel
Gron
Llys Wyfra
Lane
Englefield
Bryan Cl
Crs
Park
Dwfor
Alwen
Av
Elw
Ffordd
Ogwen
Avenue
Pen-Y-Garreg Close

2

Prenbrigog

Uwch-Y-Nant
Trem
Afon
Chambers
Mercia
Bryn Road
Wats Dyke Av
Wats Dyke Infant School
Park Av
Highfield Av
Elm
Wlk
Colliers
Overleigh Drive

Bron-Yr-Eglwys
Argoed
Llys
Wyfa
Av
Penymaes
Dedwydd
Llys
Vale Drive
Mount Close
East Close
West Vw
Mold Rd
Cwm Cl
PO
Mold
Ffordd Offa
Grays Road
Surgery
Drive
Carton Road
Mold Rd
Ellesmere Rd
Beech Gv
Mountain Vw
Pine Gv
Cr El
Pren Av
Mold Road
The Cedars
Aimal Rd
View Road
Overdale
Bod Offa Drive
Cr Y Cwm
Mayfiel Lane
Bonza

3

Bryn offa
A549
MOLD ROAD

Clwyd Av
Tir Wat
Bryn Betwen
Cr Y Cw

42

Rose Lane

Whitehouse Farm

Well

4

Tyddyn Farm

A494

A541

hen Gray
ad
ambrian
us Pk

363

5
s-major

25 26

E F G H

Llong

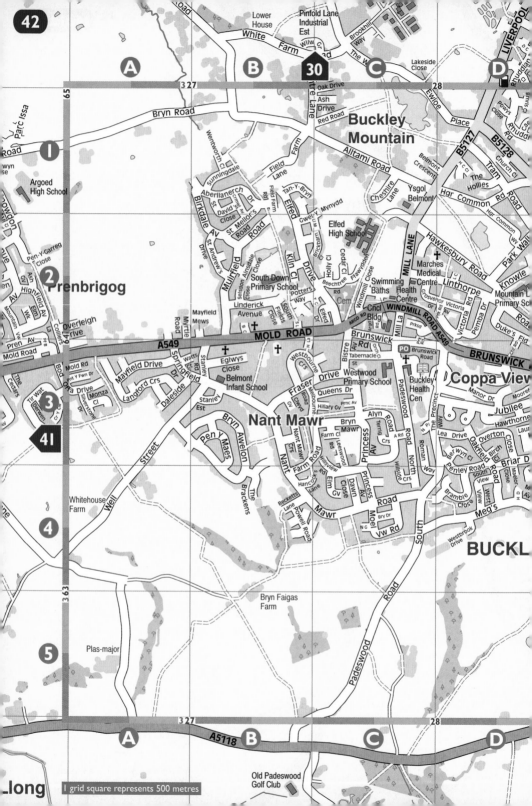

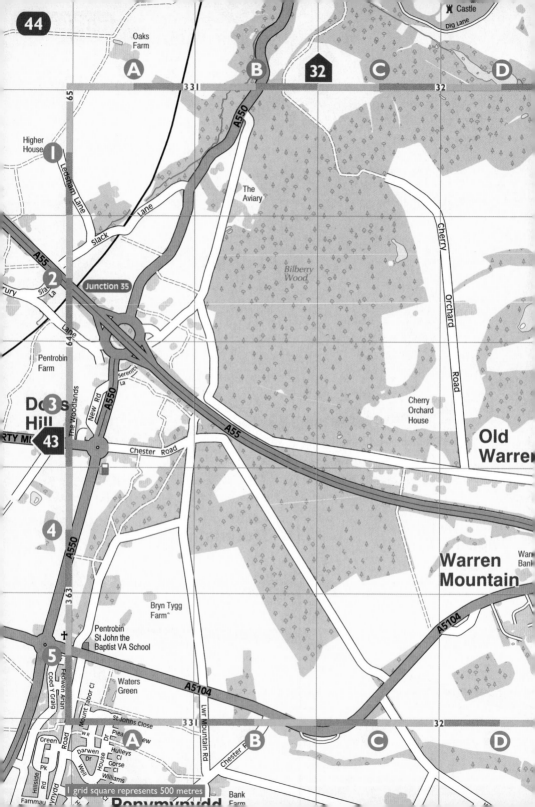

46

Hawarden Airport

A   335   **B**   **34**   **C**   36   **D**

1

Aircraft Factory

Broughton Industrial Estate

Well Ho Farm

Broughton Mills Road

2

ary's Way

CHESTER ROAD

A5104   CHESTER   ROAD

Hope's Place

Bretton Lane

A5104   CHESTER ROAD

P

Church Road

Isimonstone Rd

Bladd Cldwn

A W Watson

Simonstone Rd

El Av

Larne Dr

Broughton Shopping Park

Bretton

3

CHESTER ROAD

Eaton Close

ry Rd

A55

Rd

Sid

Broughtine Rd

Bretton Road

45

erford Rd

Madi

Congleton

Cl

Rd

w c

The Boulevard

A55

A55

Flintshire

Cheshire C

Broughton

Parkfield

Watson's Cl

Merton Rd

Melton Vale

Bracken Cl

4

A55

A55

Junction 35A

Bretton Wood

363

5

A   335   **B**   **C**   36   **D**

CH4

Gorstella

I grid square represents 500 metres

Saltney

Lache

The Lache Eyes

Decoy Farm

Chester Southerly Caravan Park

Roughill

50

H

A **B** 38 **C** **D**

65

A55

1

Caldy Valley Road

PO

Gorse Way

Speedwell Cl

Arnhem Way

Wavells Way

Kohima Crs

Promise

2

64

A55

3

49

B5130

Old Hall

4

3 63

Portersheath Farm

Heathcroft Farm

Sandy Lane

5

The Grange

Huntington Hall

A **B** **C** **D**

3 43

44

Saighton Hall Farm

Abbot's Meads	24 C5	Coppa View	42 D3	Lane End	43 E3	New Brighton	29 G4	Saughall	
Alltami	30 A4	Dobs Hill	43 H3	Lea by Backford	12 B2	Newton	25 F4	Sealand	
Aston	32 A1	Drury	43 G2	Leadmill	40 D2	Northop	17 E4	Shotton	
Backford	12 C2	Ewloe	31 G3	Little Heath	38 D4	Northop Hall	18 C5	Shotwick	
Big Mancot	32 C2	Ewloe Green	31 E2	Little Mancot	32 D2	Old Warren	44 D3	Skywin	
Blacon	23 G3	Flint	5 E3	Little Mountain	43 G4	Pentre	20 D4	Soughton	
Boughton	37 H2	Garden City	20 D2	Littleton	38 C1	Pentre	41 E3	Spon Green	
Bretton	46 B3	Golftyn	7 E5	Maes-y-dre	40 C1	Picton	14 B3	Stamford Bridge	
Bridge Trafford	15 F3	Guilden Sutton	27 E4	Mancot Royal	33 E1	Piper's Ash	26 B5	The Moor	
Broughton	45 H4	Handbridge	37 F5	Mickle Trafford	26 D1	Plemstall	15 G5	Upton	
Brown Heath	39 G1	Hawarden	32 C4	Milners Heath	51 H5	Prenbrigog	41 H2	Upton Heath	
Buckley	42 D4	Higher Shotton	19 G4	Mold	40 A2	Queen's Park	3 J6	Vicarscross	
Buckley Mountain	42 C1	Hoole	37 H1	Mollington	11 G5	Queensferry	20 C3	Warren Mountain	
Burntwood Pentre	43 E1	Hoole Bank	26 B2	Moston	13 E5	Rowton	51 E2	Waverton	
Chester	3 H5	Huntington	49 G1	Mount Pleasant	4 C3	Rowton Moor	51 E1	Wepre	
Christleton	38 D4	Kelsterton	6 C5	Mynydd Isa	41 F1	Saltney	47 F2	Wervin	
Connah's Quay	19 F1	Lache	47 H2	Nant Mawr	42 B3	Sandycroft	33 F2		

USING THE STREET INDEX

Street names are listed alphabetically. Each street name is followed by its postal town or area locality, the Postcode District, the page number, and the reference to the square in which the name is found.

Standard index entries are shown as follows:

Abbey Gn *CH/BCN* CH1 ....2 D3

Street names and selected addresses not shown on the map due to scale restrictions are shown in the index with an asterisk:

Alyn Bank *MOLD/BUCK* CH7 * 40 D2

GENERAL ABBREVIATIONS

ACC	ACCESS	CTYD	COURTYARD	HLS	HILLS	MWY	MOTORWAY	SE	SOUTH
ALY	ALLEY	CUTT	CUTTINGS	HO	HOUSE	N	NORTH	SER	SERVICE
AP	APPROACH	CV	COVE	HOL	HOLLOW	NE	NORTH EAST	SH	SH
AR	ARCADE	CYN	CANYON	HOSP	HOSPITAL	NW	NORTH WEST	SHOP	SHO
ASS	ASSOCIATION	DEPT	DEPARTMENT	HRB	HARBOUR	O/P	OVERPASS	SKWY	SK
AV	AVENUE	DL	DALE	HTH	HEATH	OFF	OFFICE	SMT	SL
BCH	BEACH	DM	DAM	HTS	HEIGHTS	ORCH	ORCHARD	SOC	SC
BLDS	BUILDINGS	DR	DRIVE	HVN	HAVEN	OV	OVAL	SP	SP
BND	BEND	DRO	DROVE	HWY	HIGHWAY	PAL	PALACE	SPR	S
BNK	BANK	DRY	DRIVEWAY	IMP	IMPERIAL	PAS	PASSAGE	SQ	SC
BR	BRIDGE	DWGS	DWELLINGS	IN	INLET	PAV	PAVILION	ST	ST
BRK	BROOK	E	EAST	IND EST	INDUSTRIAL ESTATE	PH	PUBLIC HOUSE	STN	STN
BTM	BOTTOM	EMB	EMBANKMENT	INF	INFIRMARY	PK	PARK	STN	ST
BUS	BUSINESS	EMBY	EMBASSY	INFO	INFORMATION	PKWY	PARKWAY	STRD	ST
BVD	BOULEVARD	ESP	ESPLANADE	INT	INTERCHANGE	PL	PLACE	S	SOUTH
BY	BYPASS	EST	ESTATE	IS	ISLAND	PLN	PLAIN	TDG	TR
CATH	CATHEDRAL	EX	EXCHANGE	JCT	JUNCTION	PLNS	PLAINS	TER	TEF
CEM	CEMETERY	EXPY	EXPRESSWAY	JTY	JETTY	PLZ	PLAZA	THWY	THROUG
CEN	CENTRE	EXT	EXTENSION	KG	KING	POL	POLICE STATION	TNL	TL
CFT	CROFT	F/O	FLYOVER	KNL	KNOLL	PR	PRINCE	TOLL	TL
CH	CHURCH	FC	FOOTBALL CLUB	L	LAKE	PREC	PRECINCT	TPK	TUR
CHA	CHASE	FLD	FIELD	LA	LANE	PREP	PREPARATORY	TR	
CHYD	CHURCHYARD	FLDS	FIELDS	LGT	LIGHT	PRIM	PRIMARY	TRL	
CIR	CIRCLE	FLS	FALLS	LK	LOCK	PROM	PROMENADE	TWR	T
CIRC	CIRCUS	FLS	FLATS	LKS	LAKES	PRS	PRINCESS	U/P	UNDEF
CL	CLOSE	FM	FARM	LNDG	LANDING	PT	PORT	UNI	UNIVE
CLFS	CLIFFS	FT	FORT	LTL	LITTLE	PT	POINT	UPR	L
CMP	CAMP	FWY	FREEWAY	LWR	LOWER	PTH	PATH	VA	V:
CNR	CORNER	FY	FERRY	MAG	MAGISTRATE	PZ	PIAZZA	VIAD	VIA
CO	COUNTY	GA	GATE	MAN	MANSIONS	QD	QUADRANT	VIL	
COLL	COLLEGE	GAL	GALLERY	MD	MEAD	QU	QUEEN	VIS	
COM	COMMON	GDN	GARDEN	MDW	MEADOWS	QY	QUAY	VLG	VII
COMM	COMMISSION	GDNS	GARDENS	MEM	MEMORIAL	R	RIVER	VLS	
CON	CONVENT	GLD	GLADE	MKT	MARKET	RBT	ROUNDABOUT	VW	VW
COT	COTTAGE	GLN	GLEN	MKTS	MARKETS	RD	ROAD	W	W
COTS	COTTAGES	GN	GREEN	ML	MALL	RDG	RIDGE	WD	W
CP	CAPE	GND	GROUND	ML	MILL	REP	REPUBLIC	WHF	W
CPS	COPSE	GRA	GRANGE	MNR	MANOR	RES	RESERVOIR	WKS	W
CR	CREEK	GRG	GARAGE	MS	MEWS	RFC	RUGBY FOOTBALL CLUB	WKS	W
CREM	CREMATORIUM	GT	GREAT	MSN	MISSION	RI	RISE	WY	W
CRS	CRESCENT	GTWY	GATEWAY	MT	MOUNT	RP	RAMP	YD	
CSWY	CAUSEWAY	GV	GROVE	MTN	MOUNTAIN	RW	ROW	YHA	YOUTH HC
CT	COURT	HGR	HIGHER	MTS	MOUNTAINS	S	SOUTH		
CTRL	CENTRAL	HL	HILL	MUS	MUSEUM	SCH	SCHOOL		
CTS	COURTS								

POSTCODE TOWNS AND AREA ABBREVIATIONS

CH/BCN	Chester/Blacon	CHSE	Chester southeast	CQ	Connah's Quay	FROD/HEL	Frodsham/Helsby
CHNE	Chester northeast	CHSW/BR	Chester southwest/Broughton	FLINT	Flint	MOLD/BUCK	Mold/Buckley

A

Aberllanerch Dr		**Alderberry Rd** *CQ* CH5 ....31 G5	**Alvis Rd** *CQ* CH5 ....33 G1	**Anfield Cl** *CQ* CH5 ....
MOLD/BUCK CH7 ....42 B1	**Alder Gv** *CHNE* CH2 ....26 A5	**Alwen Av** *MOLD/BUCK* CH7 ....41 H2	**Anne's Wy** *CHSW/BR* CH4....
Aber Rd *FLINT* CH6 ....4 C2	**Alderley Pl** *CH/BCN* CH1 ....23 H3	**Alwen Dr** *CQ* CH5 ....19 F3	**Anvil Cl** *CH/BCN* CH1 .....
Aber Vw *CQ* CH5 ....18 D1	**Aldford Rd** *CHNE* CH2 ....25 G3	**Alwyn Cl** *MOLD/BUCK* CH7 ....40 B1	**Appleby Dr** *CQ* CH5 ......
Abingdon Crs *CHSW/BR* CH4 ..48 A1	**Aled Crs** *FLINT* CH6 ....4 A5	**Alwyn Gdns** *CHNE* CH2 ....25 F1	**Appleton Rd** *CHNE* CH2 ....
Acres La *CHNE* CH2 ....3 C2	**Aled Wy** *CHSW/BR* CH4........47 G2	**Alyn Bank** *MOLD/BUCK* CH7 * ...40 D2	**Appleyards La** *CHSW/BR* CH4 .
Adder Hl *CHSE* CH3 ....38 A5	**Alexandra Rd** *MOLD/BUCK* CH7 ..40 C3	**Alyndale Av** *MOLD/BUCK* CH7 ..41 G3	**Aran Cl** *MOLD/BUCK* CH7 ...
Adelaide Rd *CH/BCN* CH1 .....23 C5	**Alexandra St** *CQ* CH5 ....20 A3	**Alyndale Rd** *CHSW/BR* CH4 ....47 E5	**Archers Wy** *CH/BCN* CH1 ...
Adwy Wynt *FLINT* CH6 ....5 E5	**Allans Cl** *CQ* CH5 ....20 B4	**Alyn Pk** *CQ* CH5 ....31 C4	**Archway** *MOLD/BUCK* CH7 .
Ael y Bryn *CHNE* CH2 ....36 D1	**Allansford Av** *CHSE* CH3 ....51 F3	**Alyn Rd** *CHNE* CH2 ....15 E5	**Argoed Av** *MOLD/BUCK* CH7 ..
Afon Vw *CQ* CH5 ....18 D1	**Allington La** *CHSW/BR* CH4 .....37 F5	*MOLD/BUCK* CH7 ....42 C3	**Argoed Cl** *MOLD/BUCK* CH7 ..
Agenoria Cl *CQ* CH5 ....18 D1	**Allington Pl** *CHSW/BR* CH4 .....37 F5	**Alyn St** *MOLD/BUCK* CH7 ......40 D2	**Argoed Rd** *MOLD/BUCK* CH7 ..
Ainsdale Cl *MOLD/BUCK* CH7 ...42 B2	**Alltami Rd** *MOLD/BUCK* CH7 ....30 A5	**Alyn Vw** *MOLD/BUCK* CH7 * 40 D2	**Argoed Vw** *MOLD/BUCK* CH7 ..
Airfield Vw *CHSW/BR* CH4 .....45 G1	**Allt Goch** *FLINT* CH6 ....4 D3	**Ambleside Av** *CHSE* CH3 ......25 C5	**Argyll Av** *CHSW/BR* CH4 ....
Albert Av *FLINT* CH6 ....5 E4	**Allt-goch La** *FLINT* CH6 ....17 E1	**Ambleside Cl** *CQ* CH5 ....18 D2	**Arley Cl** *CHNE* CH2 ....
Albert St *CH/BCN* CH1 ....3 G2	**Alma St** *CHSE* CH3 ....3 K3	**Ambrose Ter**	**Arnhem Wy** *CHSE* CH3 .....
Albion Pl *CH/BCN* CH1 ....2 E6	**Alpraham Crs** *CHNE* CH2 ....25 F3	*MOLD/BUCK* CH7 * 40 D3	**Arnold Gv** *CQ* CH5 ....
Albion St *CH/BCN* CH1 ....2 E5	**Alun Cl** *MOLD/BUCK* CH7 ......18 A5	**The Anchorage** *CHSE* CH3 .....51 E4	**Arnold's Crs** *CHSW/BR* CH4 .
Aberdaron Dr	**Alun Crs** *CHSW/BR* CH4 ....48 B1	**Andrew Crs** *CHSW/BR* CH4 .....3 H7	**Arradon Ct** *CHNE* CH2 .....
CH/BCN CH1.................35 H1	**Alder Av** *CQ* CH5 ....31 H1		**Arrowcroft Rd** *CHSE* CH3 ....
Aber Las *FLINT* CH6 ....5 E5			

st CH/BCN CH1 ....36 B2
nk CHSE CH3 * 26 B5
Pl CHNE CH2 ....25 F5
rnsdale Dr CQ CH5 ....33 E1
MOLD/BUCK CH7 ....
t Crs CH/BCN CH1 ....23 C4
....32 C2
Rd CQ CH5 ....20 A3
/BUCK CH7 ....48 C2
H5 ....20 A3
/D/BUCK CH7 ....40 B2
y La CHNE CH2 ....14 B5
e CH5 ....14 B5
Cl CQ CH5 ....32 C3
wn Ct CHNE CH2 ....24 D5
c CQ CH5 ....20 B5
FLINT CH6 ....5 F4
rd Rd CH/BCN CH1 ....23 F5
Cl CQ CH5 ....31 F5
Crs CHSW/BR CH4 ....49 E1
on Wy CHSW/BR CH4 ....46 A3
t CQ CH5 ....11 F4
enue CQ CH5 ....32 B4
LD/BUCK CH7 ....40 D5
ct CQ CH5 ....19 E3
LD/BUCK CH7 ....40 D4
ale Rd CHSW/BR CH4 ....43 E3
ea Cl CHSW/BR CH4 ....47 H3

B

ge Rd CQ CH5 ....21 F5
e Av CHNE CH2 ....24 D4
Dr CHNE CH2 ....25 E4
field Av CHSE CH3 ....49 C1
Hall Ct CHNE CH2 ....24 D4
or's La CHSE CH3 ....37 H4
Queen St CH/BCN CH1 ....3 C5
rs Cl CHSE CH3 ....38 D5
ers Rd CQ CH5 ....19 E4
ers Wk CHNE CH2 ....13 F4
Bridge Cl CHNE CH2 ....38 D5
Wy CHSE CH3 ....38 D5
rer Crs CHSE CH3 ....38 A2
ral Cl FLINT CH6 ....4 D6
ral Pk CH/BCN CH1 ....24 C5
Cl CHNE CH2 ....25 F4
La MOLD/BUCK CH7 ....45 G4
d Rd CQ CH5 ....7 E5
Rw MOLD/BUCK CH7 ....43 E3
Rd CQ CH5 ....32 C3
Vls MOLD/BUCK CH7 ....40 C2
el La MOLD/BUCK CH7 ....43 F4
cov Cl CHNE CH2 ....31 H5
Hill Rd CHSE CH3 ....37 H2
y Cft CHSE CH3 ....37 H5
outh Cl CQ CH5 ....18 D2
ss Cl CH/BCN CH1 ....24 A3
arnyard CQ CH5 ....32 A1
bins La FLINT CH6 ....4 D5
omont Cl CH/BCN CH1 ....31 H3
ny Wy CHSW/BR CH4 ....47 H3
d Well Hl CHSE CH3 ....4 D5
ears CH/BCN CH1 ....3 G4
olemew Wy
HSW/BR CH4 ....48 D1
el Cl CQ CH5 ....21 E3
et CH/BCN CH1 ....3 C5
onsfield Rd CQ CH5 ....3 H4
onsfield St CHSE CH3 ....3 H4
maris Cl MOLD/BUCK CH7 ....42 A4
mont Cl CHSW/BR CH4 ....41 H1
ett's La CHSE CH3 ....42 B4
/BUCK CH7 ....42 B4
ood Wy MOLD/BUCK CH7 ....40 B2
ward Rw CHNE CH2 ....24 D4
Beeches CHNE CH4 * 34 A4
H5 ....31 G5
h Gv CHNE CH2 ....37 H1
OLD/BUCK CH7 ....41 H2
hlands Av CHSE CH3 ....31 H1
mont CHSW/BR CH4 ....45 G4
htree Rd MOLD/BUCK CH7 ....42 C2
chway CHNE CH2 ....19 E2
chwood Cl CQ CH5 ....40 D5
chwood Rd MOLD/BUCK CH7 .40 B1
chwood Rd CHSW/BR CH4 ......47 D2
mton Pathway
HSW/BR CH4 ....37 F5
ston Rd CHSW/BR CH4 ....45 G4
lston Vw CHSW/BR CH4 ....47 H1
rave Av CHNE CH2 ....25 E5
rave Rd CHSE CH3 ....38 A4
rave St CHSE CH3 ....38 A4
evue La CHSE CH3 ....26 C5
mont Av CQ CH5 ....37 H1
mont Crs MOLD/BUCK CH7 .....47 E1
emont Dr CHSW/BR CH4 ....48 B1
vedere Cl CQ CH5 ....33 H5
edere Dr CH/BCN CH1 ....23 H5
lech Cl CQ CH5 ....18 D2

Bennett's La CQ CH5 ....32 A2
Benton Dr CHNE CH2 ....24 D5
Berkley Dr CHSW/BR CH4 ....49 F1
Bernsdale Cl CQ CH5 ....33 E1
Berwyn Cl MOLD/BUCK CH7 ....41 H1
MOLD/BUCK CH7 ....42 D3
Bewley Ct CHSE CH3 ....37 H5
Bidston Cl CHNE CH2 ....25 E4
Birch Cl MOLD/BUCK CH7 ....42 D3
The Birches CHSW/BR CH4 ......45 G4
Birchfield Crs CQ CH5 ....32 A1
Birch Heath La CHSE CH3 ....38 D4
Birch Rdg FLINT CH6 ....5 E3
Birch Ri CHNE CH2 ....25 E3
CHSW/BR CH4 ....25 E3
Birch Rd CHSW/BR CH4 ....48 A2
Birkdale Av CHSW/BR CH4 ....42 B1
Bishops Cl CHSE CH3 ....41 H3
Bishops Ga CHNE CH2 ....37 G1
Bishop St CHNE CH2 ....37 G1
Bistre Av MOLD/BUCK CH7 ......42 C3
Bistre Cl MOLD/BUCK CH7 ....42 C3
Black Brk MOLD/BUCK CH7 ......28 C3
Blackbrook Av CQ CH5 ....3 F5
Black Diamond St CH/BCN CH1 .5 E3
Black Friars CHNE CH2 ....2 D6
Blackthorn Cl CHSE CH3 ....49 H2
CHSW/BR CH4 ....45 G4
Blacon Av CH/BCN CH1 ....24 A4
Blacon Hall Rd CH/BCN CH1 ....24 A4
Blacon Point Rd CH/BCN CH1 ..35 G1
Blake Cl CQ CH5 ....31 H3
Blenheim Ct CQ CH5 ....31 H3
Bluebell Cl CHSE CH3 ....50 A1
Bodlondeb FLINT CH6 ....5 E5
Bodnant Gv CQ CH5 ....19 E3
Bod Offa Dr MOLD/BUCK CH7 ..42 D3
Bold Pl FLINT CH6 ....2 D5
Bold Sq CH/BCN CH1 ....2 E5
Bolesworth Rd CHNE CH2 ....25 G3
Boleyn Cl CH/BCN CH1 ....5 F2
Bollam Cl CQ CH5 ....18 D1
Border Wy CHSE CH3 ....38 B3
Borough Gv FLINT CH6 ....5 E5
Bottoms La CHSW/BR CH4 ....3 H7
Boughton CHSE CH3 ....3 J4
Boughton Hall Av CHSE CH3 .....37 H3
Boughton Hall Rd CHSE CH3 ....38 A3
The Boulevard CHSW/BR CH4 ..45 H4
Boundary La CHSW/BR CH4 .....47 C2
Bouverie St CH/BCN CH1 ....2 C1
Boxmoor Cl CHSW/BR CH4 ......48 D2
Bracken Cl CHSW/BR CH4 ....45 H4
Brackendale Rd CQ CH5 ....32 C1
The Brackens MOLD/BUCK CH7 42 B4
Bradford St CH/BCN CH1 ....3 G5
Bradshaw Av CHSW/BR CH4 ....45 G4
Braemar Cl CHSE CH3 ....38 B1
Braeside Av CQ CH5 ....32 B2
Bramble Cl CHSE CH3 ....37 H5
MOLD/BUCK CH7 ....42 C1
The Brambles CQ CH5 ....20 A3
Bramley Wy CQ CH5 ....37 H5
Brassey St CHSE CH3 ....3 K4
Bray Rd CHSW/BR CH4 ....48 A1
Breeze Hl CQ CH5 ....19 C2
Brennus Pl CH/BCN CH1 ....2 C3
Brentwood Rd CH/BCN CH1 .....23 H4
Breton Cl CHSE CH3 ....25 F4
Bretton Dr CHSW/BR CH4 ....45 G4
Bretton La CHSW/BR CH4 ....46 C2
Bretton Rd CHSW/BR CH4 ....46 B3
Briar Dr MOLD/BUCK CH7 ....42 D4
Brickbarn Cl MOLD/BUCK CH7 .42 C2
Brickfields CHSE CH3 ....43 E5
Bridge Dr CHSE CH3 ....3 J5
Bridgeman Rd CH/BCN CH1 .....35 H1
Bridge Pl CH/BCN CH1 ....2 E6
Bridge St CH/BCN CH1 ....2 E5
CHSW/BR CH4 ....35 C5
CQ CH5 ....19 H2
MOLD/BUCK CH7 ....40 D2
Bridge Street Rw East
CH/BCN CH1 ....2 E5
Bridge Street Rw West
CH/BCN CH1 ....2 D5
Bridge Vw CQ CH5 ....21 E2
Bridgewater Dr CHSE CH3 ....38 B2
Brisbane Rd CH/BCN CH1 ....23 F5
Bristol Cl CQ CH5 ....23 F5
Broadmead CHSE CH3 ....38 B2
Broad Oak Av CHSW/BR CH4 ...45 F4
Broad Oak Cl CQ CH5 ....19 E3
Broadway CQ CH5 ....31 F2
CQ CH5 ....31 F2
Broadway Av CHNE CH2 ....25 F4
Broadway West CHNE CH2 ....25 E4
Bro Alun MOLD/BUCK CH7 ......40 C2
Bro Deg FLINT CH6 ....4 C6
Brodie Cl CHNE CH2 ....25 F4
Bromfield Cl MOLD/BUCK CH7 .40 D4
Bromfield Pk MOLD/BUCK CH7 40 D4
Broncoed La MOLD/BUCK CH7 40 C5
Broncoed Pk MOLD/BUCK CH7 40 C5
Broncoed Ter
MOLD/BUCK CH7 * 40 D5
Bron Uwyn FLINT CH6 ....4 C6
Bronte Gv CQ CH5 ....31 H4
Bron y Nant MOLD/BUCK CH7 .40 D5
Bron-yr-Eglwys
MOLD/BUCK CH7 ....41 F3
Brookdale Av CQ CH5 ....19 F3
FLINT CH6 ....4 C5
Brookdale Wy CHSE CH3 ....51 G2
Brooke Av CHNE CH2 ....25 E4
Brooke Cl CQ CH5 ....31 F4
Brookhill Wy MOLD/BUCK CH7 .30 C5
Brook La CHNE CH2 ....3 H4
Brookleigh Av CHSE CH3 ....32 C2
Brookmoore Ct CHNE CH2 ....36 D1

Brook Pl CH/BCN CH1 ....3 F2
Brook Rd CQ CH5 ....19 H3
Brookside CHSE CH3 ....37 H4
CQ CH5 ....20 D2
Brookside Ter CHNE CH2 ....25 E5
Brook St CH/BCN CH1 ....16 D4
MOLD/BUCK CH7 ....40 D3
MOLD/BUCK CH7 ....40 C3
MOLD/BUCK CH7 ....43 E3
Brook Street Br CHNE CH2 ....3 H1
CHNE CH2 ....3 H1
Broughton Hall Rd
CHSW/BR CH4 ....45 H4
Broughton Mills Rd
CHSW/BR CH4 ....46 C1
Brown Heath Rd CHSE CH3 ......39 F5
Browning Cl CH/BCN CH1 ....24 A4
Brown's La CHSW/BR CH4 ....36 D5
Brunswick Rd MOLD/BUCK CH7 42 C3
Brunswood Gn CQ CH5 ....31 G4
Brushwood Av FLINT CH6 ....4 C5
Bryan Gv MOLD/BUCK CH7 ......41 G2
Bryn Awelon MOLD/BUCK CH7 40 D1
Bryn Cae CQ CH5 ....5 E2
Bryn Clwyd MOLD/BUCK CH7 ..41 G1
Bryn Coch Crs MOLD/BUCK CH7 40 D1
Bryn Coch La MOLD/BUCK CH7 40 D1
Bryn Coch Uchaf
MOLD/BUCK CH7 ....40 A4
Bryn-coed-Wepre CQ CH5 ....18 D5
Bryn Derw FLINT CH6 ....5 E5
Bryn Derwen MOLD/BUCK CH7 41 H3
Bryn Dr CQ CH5 ....32 B2
Bryn Eithin CQ CH5 ....18 D4
Bryn Garmon MOLD/BUCK CH7 40 D1
Bryn Gwyn FLINT CH6 ....5 E5
Bryn-gwyn La MOLD/BUCK CH7 18 A4
Bryn Helig FLINT CH6 ....5 E5
Bryn Heulog MOLD/BUCK CH7 .40 D1
Bryn Hilyn La MOLD/BUCK CH7 40 A4
Bryn Hyfryd MOLD/BUCK CH7 ..40 D1
MOLD/BUCK CH7 ....28 D5
Bryn La MOLD/BUCK CH7 ....40 D5
Bryn Mawr MOLD/BUCK CH7 ...42 C3
Bryn Mor Dr FLINT CH6 ....4 C3
Bryn Noddfa MOLD/BUCK CH7 .40 D1
Bryn Offa MOLD/BUCK CH7 .....41 H3
Bryn Onnen FLINT CH6 ....5 E5
Bryn Rhyd MOLD/BUCK CH7 ....18 D5
Bryn Rd CQ CH5 ....19 E1
FLINT CH6 ....5 E5
MOLD/BUCK CH7 ....42 A1
Bryn Seion La MOLD/BUCK CH7 40 D1
Bryn Siriol FLINT CH6 ....5 E5
Bryn Teg MOLD/BUCK CH7 ......28 D5
Brynwood Dr MOLD/BUCK CH7 42 C4
Bryn-y-Baal Rd
MOLD/BUCK CH7 ....41 G1
Buckingham Av CHSE CH3 ....37 H5
Bulkeley St CHSE CH3 ....37 H3
Bumpers La CH/BCN CH1 * 36 A3
Bunce St CH/BCN CH1 ....2 D6
Burges St CHNE CH2 ....37 G1
Burnham Rd CHSW/BR CH4 .....48 A1
Burns Cl CQ CH5 ....31 F5
Burns Wy CH/BCN CH1 ....23 H3
Burntwood Ct MOLD/BUCK CH7 40 C5
Burntwood Rd
MOLD/BUCK CH7 ....43 F1
Burton Rd CH/BCN CH1 ....18 D5
Bush Rd CHSE CH3 ....38 D5
Butler St CQ CH5 ....20 A4
Butterbache Rd CHSE CH3 ....49 H1
Butterbur Cl CHSE CH3 ....49 H1
Buttermere Cl CQ CH5 ....18 D2
Byron Cl CHSE CH3 ....23 H3
CQ CH5 ....31 F4
CQ CH5 ....31 F4
Bythom Cl CHSE CH3 ....38 D5

C

Cable St CQ CH5 ....19 F1
Cadnant Cl CH/BCN CH1 ....35 G1
Cadnant Ct CHSW/BR CH4 ....38 A2
Cae Bracty MOLD/BUCK CH7 ...40 C3
Cae Bychan FLINT CH6 ....5 E4
Cae Derw FLINT CH6 ....5 E4
Cae Glas MOLD/BUCK CH7 .....29 E3
MOLD/BUCK CH7 ....40 B3
Cae Haf MOLD/BUCK CH7 ....18 B5
Cae Hir FLINT CH6 ....5 E4
MOLD/BUCK CH7 ....40 B3
Cae Isa MOLD/BUCK CH7 ....29 F5
Cae Llys CQ CH5 ....18 D4
Caernarvon Cl CQ CH5 ....40 D1
Caerphilly Rd MOLD/BUCK CH7 18 C5
Caesar Av FLINT CH6 ....5 F4
Cairndale Av CQ CH5 ....19 E2
Cairns Crs CH/BCN CH1 ....18 G5
Caldbeck Crs CQ CH5 ....18 D2
Caldas Cl CQ CH5 ....18 D3
Caldy Av CQ CH5 ....28 E3
Caldy Cl CHNE CH2 ....25 E4
Caldy Valley Rd CHSE CH3 ....49 H1
Cambrian Av CHSE CH3 ....38 A2
Cambrian Cl CQ CH5 ....19 F2
MOLD/BUCK CH7 ....24 B2
Cambrian Wy CQ CH5 ....31 H2
Cambridge Rd CHNE CH2 ....25 G4
Campion Cl CHSE CH3 ....49 H1
Camrose Cl CQ CH5 ....18 D2
Canadian Av CHNE CH2 ....25 H5
Canal Side CH/BCN CH1 ....3 G3
Canal St CH/BCN CH1 ....2 E5

Canberra Wy CH/BCN CH1 ....23 G5
Canning St CH/BCN CH1 ....2 D3
Canol y Bryn MOLD/BUCK CH7 41 H1
Canterbury Rd CH/BCN CH1 .....24 A4
Capeland Cl CHSW/BR CH4 ......47 H2
Capenhurst Rd CHSE CH3 ....51 G2
Carlines Av CQ CH5 ....31 H2
Carlisle Rd CH/BCN CH1 ....23 H4
Carlton Av CHSW/BR CH4 ....47 G1
Carlton Cl CHNE CH2 ....26 D1
Carlton Pl CHNE CH2 ....25 H5
Carmel Cl CHSW/BR CH4 ....36 B5
Carter St CH/BCN CH1 ....3 G2
Carton Rd MOLD/BUCK CH7 ....41 G3
Castle Cl CHSW/BR CH4 ....45 G1
Castle Croft Rd CHSE CH3 ....48 C2
Castle Dr CQ CH5 ....2 D7
Castle Dyke St FLINT CH6 ....5 E5
Castle Hill St CQ CH5 ....20 A5
Castle Park Av CQ CH5 ....18 D4
Castle Ri CQ CH5 ....2 E6
Castle Sq MOLD/BUCK CH7 .....5 E2
Castle St CH/BCN CH1 ....2 D6
FLINT CH6 ....5 E2
Catherine Dr CQ CH5 ....31 H2
Catherine St CHNE CH2 ....2 B3
Caughall Rd CHNE CH2 ....25 F1
Cavalier Dr CHSE CH3 ....2 D7
Cavendish Rd CHSW/BR CH4 ...36 C5
Cawdor Dr CHSE CH3 ....37 H2
Cecil St CHSE CH3 ....37 H3
Cedar Av CQ CH5 ....6 D5
CQ CH5 ....21 F2
Cedar Cl MOLD/BUCK CH7 ....42 C2
Cedar Ct CHNE CH2 ....20 D3
Cedar Gdns CQ CH5 ....31 H1
Cedar Gv CHSW/BR CH4 ....26 A5
MOLD/BUCK CH7 ....40 B2
Cedar Ms MOLD/BUCK CH7 .....23 H5
Cedar Pk CHSE CH3 ....38 B2
The Cedars MOLD/BUCK CH7 ..18 D4
Cefna Cl CQ CH5 ....18 D4
Cefn Rd CQ CH5 ....19 E1
Celandine Cl CHSE CH3 ....37 H5
Celtic St CHSE CH3 ....19 H2
Celyn Av CQ CH5 ....18 D4
Celyn Crs CHSW/BR CH4 ....42 G2
Celyn Maes MOLD/BUCK CH7 ..16 C3
Cement Pl CH/BCN CH1 * 35 H1
Cemlyn Cl CQ CH5 ....20 A4
Central Dr CQ CH5 ....19 C1
Cestrian St CQ CH5 ....
Chain Maker's Rw
CHSW/BR CH4 ....35 H5
Challinor St CHSE CH3 ....37 H3
Chambers La MOLD/BUCK CH7 41 G2
Chandos Cl MOLD/BUCK CH7 ..49 F1
Chapel Cl CH/BCN CH1 ....10 D5
CQ CH5 ....51 F2
Chapel La CHSE CH3 ....19 F2
FLINT CH6 ....4 D5
MOLD/BUCK CH7 ....3 H7
Chapel St CH/BCN CH1 ....3 F2
CHSW/BR CH4 ....3 J1
MOLD/BUCK CH7 ....40 D5
Charlotte St CH/BCN CH1 ....2 B3
Charterhall Dr CHNE CH2 ....3 J3
Chaser Cl MOLD/BUCK CH7 .....36 A1
Chatsworth Dr CHNE CH2 ....25 H4
Chaucer Cl CH/BCN CH1 ....23 H3
Chemistry La CQ CH5 ....5 H5
Cheriton Cl MOLD/BUCK CH7 ...18 D5
Cherry Dale Rd CHSW/BR CH4 45 F4
Cherry Grove Rd CHSE CH3 .....37 H3
Cherry Orchard Rd CQ CH5 ......31 F4
Cherry Rd CHSE CH3 ....37 H5
Chesham St CH/BCN CH1 * 3 G2
Cheshire La MOLD/BUCK CH7 ..37 F5
Cheshire Vw CHSW/BR CH4 .....37 E5
Chester Ap CHSW/BR CH4 ....49 E5
Chester Cl CQ CH5 ....20 A4
Chester Rd CHSE CH3 ....45 F2
CHSW/BR CH4 ....46 C2
CHSW/BR CH4 ....47 E5
CQ CH5 ....5 E2
MOLD/BUCK CH7 ....43 E3
MOLD/BUCK CH7 ....43 E3
Chester Rd (East) CQ CH5 ....20 D4
Chester Rd (West) CQ CH5 ....24 D4
Chester St CQ CH5 ....36 A5
FLINT CH6 ....5 E2
MOLD/BUCK CH7 ....40 D3
Chesterton Av CQ CH5 ....31 F4
Chesterton Dr CHNE CH2 ....25 H4
Chestnut Cl CHNE CH2 ....24 C4
FLINT CH6 ....5 E4
MOLD/BUCK CH7 ....42 C1
Chestnut Crs CQ CH5 ....31 G5
Chestnut Gv CQ CH5 ....40 A4
Chevron Hey CH/BCN CH1 ....20 A5
Chevrons Wy CH/BCN CH1 ....20 A5
Cheyney Wy CH/BCN CH1 ....2 B1
Chichester St CH/BCN CH1 ....2 C3
Chiltern Cl CH/BCN CH1 ....19 E3
CQ CH5 ....31 F5
Chirk Cl CHNE CH2 ....19 F3
Christleton Cl CHSE CH3 ....37 H3
Church Cl MOLD/BUCK CH7 .....41 G1
MOLD/BUCK CH7 ....23 H5
Church College Cl CH/BCN CH1 36 C1
Church Hall Cl CH/BCN CH1 ......24 A5
Church Hl CQ CH5 ....19 F1

Churchill Cl CQ CH5 ....31 H4
CHSE CH3 ....27 E5
CQ CH5 ....31 G1
CQ CH5 ....32 C4
MOLD/BUCK CH7 ....40 C2
Church La CHNE CH2 ....25 E2
CHSE CH3 ....27 E5
CQ CH5 ....31 G1
CQ CH5 ....32 C4
MOLD/BUCK CH7 ....40 C2
Church Rd CH/BCN CH1 ....10 D5
CHSW/BR CH4 ....45 H3
CHSW/BR CH4 ....49 F5
CQ CH5 ....19 F1
CQ CH5 ....19 E1
MOLD/BUCK CH7 ....43 E2
Church St CH/BCN CH1 ....19 E1
FLINT CH6 ....4 D3
Church Vw CQ CH5 ....33 E1
Church Wks CHSE CH3 ....38 D4
Churchward Cl CHNE CH2 ....25 E5
Church Wy CHNE CH2 ....25 E5
Churton St CHSE CH3 ....27 E4
Cinder Cl CHSE CH3 ....27 E4
Cinder La CHSE CH3 ....27 E4
Circular Dr CHSW/BR CH4 ....47 H5
City Rd CH/BCN CH1 ....15 F2
City Walls Rd CH/BCN CH1 ....2 E3
City Walls Rd CH/BCN CH1 ....2 E3
Clair Av CQ CH5 ....33 F1
Claremont Av CQ CH5 ....20 D3
Clarence Av CHSE CH3 ....38 A2
Clarence St CQ CH5 ....20 D3
Clarendon Cl CHSW/BR CH4 ....49 F1
Clay La CQ CH5 ....20 B5
Claypits La CHSE CH3 ....51 E3
Clayton Cl MOLD/BUCK CH7 ....40 B3
Clayton Rd MOLD/BUCK CH7 ...40 B3
Cleaver Rd CH/BCN CH1 ....23 H5
Cledwen Dr MOLD/BUCK CH7 ..41 H2
Cledwen Road CHSW/BR CH4 ..20 D3
Cleveland Ov CQ CH5 ....20 D3
Cleves Cl CH/BCN CH1 ....23 G3
Clifford Dr CHSW/BR CH4 ....48 A2
Clifton Dr CQ CH5 ....35 H1
Cliveden Rd CH/BCN CH1 ....24 A4
Clivedon Rd CQ CH5 ....18 D5
Clos Coed CQ CH5 ....20 D5
The Close CH/BCN CH1 ....10 D5
CQ CH5 ....11 H3
CQ CH5 ....32 A3
MOLD/BUCK CH7 ....40 B4
Clos Lindum MOLD/BUCK CH7 .5 H5
Clos y Meillion CQ CH5 ....31 G4
Clover La CHSW/BR CH4 ....48 A2
Cloverfi Pl CHSE CH3 ....48 A2
Clwyd Av CHSW/BR CH4 ....45 G1
Clwyd Cl CHSW/BR CH4 ....41 G1
Clwyd Crs MOLD/BUCK CH7 ....42 B3
Clwyd Gv MOLD/BUCK CH7 .....42 B3
Clwyd St CQ CH5 ....20 A5
Clydesdale Rd MOLD/BUCK CH7 43 G2
Coalpit La MOLD/BUCK CH7 ....11 F3
Coatings By-Pass Rd CQ CH5 ...7 G4
Coatings Two CQ CH5 ....7 G4
The Cobbles CHSW/BR CH4 .....37 E5
Coed Barfi FLINT CH6 ....4 C4
Coed Onn Rd FLINT CH6 ....5 F5
Coed Terfin CHSW/BR CH4 ....43 H5
Coed y Graig CHSW/BR CH4 .....43 H5
Colchester Sq CHSW/BR CH4 ..48 A2
Colehill Pl CQ CH5 ....7 E5
Coleridge Cl CH/BCN CH1 ....24 B4
Coleshill Rd CHSE CH3 ....4 D3
Colomendy Av CHSW/BR CH4 ..37 E5
College Gn CHSW/BR CH4 ....37 E5
College Vw CQ CH5 ....6 D5
Collfeld La MOLD/BUCK CH7 ....32 C1
Colliery La CQ CH5 ....32 C1
Coltsfoot Cl CHSE CH3 ....49 H2
Columbine Cl CHSE CH3 ....49 H1
Commonhall St CH/BCN CH1 ....2 D5
Common La CHSE CH3 ....51 E5
Compton Pl CHSW/BR CH4 ....44 B1
Congleton Rd CHSE CH3 ....45 H3
Coniston Cl CQ CH5 ....18 D3
Coniston Rd CH/BCN CH1 ....25 G4
Connah's Quay Rd
MOLD/BUCK CH7 ....17 F4
Connaught Av CQ CH5 ....20 A3
Coniston Dr MOLD/BUCK CH7 ..42 D2
Conway Av MOLD/BUCK CH7 ...43 E4
Conway Cl CQ CH5 ....47 C2
FLINT CH6 ....4 C5
Conway Ct CQ CH5 ....18 D2
Conway St MOLD/BUCK CH7 ....40 C2
Copes Cft CHSE CH3 ....37 H5
Cooper's La CQ CH5 ....7 E5
Copeswood Cl CHSW/BR CH4 ..45 H4
Coppack Cl CQ CH5 ....18 D4
Coppafield Cl MOLD/BUCK CH7 43 E3
Coppa Gv MOLD/BUCK CH7 .....43 H4
Copper Beach Cl CHSW/BR CH4 45 H4
The Coppice CQ CH5 ....31 G2
Coppins Cl CHSE CH3 ....37 H2
The Copse CQ CH5 ....31 G4
Cornist Dr FLINT CH6 ....4 C3
Cornist Rd FLINT CH6 ....4 C3
Cornwall Rd CHSE CH3 ....25 F2
Cornwall St CH/BCN CH1 ....2 A5
Coronation Rd CHSW/BR CH4 ..45 G4
Coronation St FLINT CH6 ....36 A5
Corporation St FLINT CH6 ....18 D4
Coron y Bryn MOLD/BUCK CH7 18 D4
Cotebrook Dr CHNE CH2 ....25 F2
Cotes Pl CH/BCN CH1 ....35 H1
Cotgreaves Cl CHSE CH3 ....48 C2
Cotswold Cl CHSE CH3 ....25 G5
Cottage Gdns MOLD/BUCK CH7 31 G4
Cottage La CQ CH5 ....32 C2
Cottage Rd CHSW/BR CH4 ....48 C2
Cotterill Cl CQ CH5 ....19 E4

Cotton La CHSE CH3 .....39 H2
Countess Wy CH/BCN CH1 .....24 D5
Courbet Dr CO CH5 .....18 D1
Courtland Dr CO CH5 .....31 H1
Courtney Rd CHSW/BR CH4 .....47 H5
Cousens Wy CH/BCN CH1 .....24 C5
Cowhey Cl CHSW/BR CH4 .....48 C2
Cowthorne St CHSE CH3 .....51 F2
Crabwall Pl CH/BCN CH1 .....24 A4
Craithie Rd CHSE CH3 .....37 H2
Cranbrook Cl CO CH5 .....19 F3
Cranford Ct CHSW/BR CH4 .....48 B2
Cranleigh Crs CH/BCN CH1 .....24 C5
Crawford's Wk CHNE CH2 .....3 J1
The Crescent CHNE CH2 .....25 E5
Crewe St CH/BCN CH1 .....3 G2
Criccoth Cl MOLD/BUCK CH7 .....30 D5
Croes Atti La FLINT CH6 .....5 E5
Croft Av CO CH5 .....19 F3
Croft Cl CHSE CH3 .....51 F2
Crofters Pk CO CH5 .....33 F1
Crofters Wy CH/BCN CH1 .....22 C1
  CO CH5 .....32 D2
The Croft CHNE CH2 .....25 E5
Cromwell Av MOLD/BUCK CH7 .....42 B1
Cromwell Cl CO CH5 .....31 H4
Crookenden Cl CHNE CH2 .....12 D5
Crookenden Rd CHNE CH2 .....12 D5
Crook St CH/BCN CH1 .....2 D4
Cross Ct CHNE CH2 .....25 F3
Cross Hey CHSW/BR CH4 .....3 H7
Crossley Crs CHNE CH2 .....26 A4
  CO CH5 .....3 K3
Cross Tree Ct CO CH5 .....31 E4
Cross Tree Ri CO CH5 .....31 E4
Crosstree La CO CH5 .....32 C3
Crossways CO CH5 .....31 G2
Crossways Cl CO CH5 .....20 A4
  CO CH5 .....32 D1
Crud-y-Cwynt MOLD/BUCK CH7 .....41 H5
Cunliffe St MOLD/BUCK CH7 .....40 C4
Curzon St CH/BCN CH1 .....2 D5
Curzon Cl CHSW/BR CH4 .....B4 B4
Curzon Pk North CHSW/BR CH4 .....2 A7
Curzon St CH/BCN CH1 .....36 A5
Cwm Cl MOLD/BUCK CH7 .....41 G3
Cwm Eithion FLINT CH6 .....5 E5
Cwrt Erwain CHSW/BR CH4 * 35 H5
Cwrt Leighton CO CH5 .....19 F1
Cwrt Onnen CO CH5 .....32 D2
Cyman Cl CH/BCN CH1 .....35 G1

D

Dafydd Cl MOLD/BUCK CH7 .....41 H1
Daisy Hill Rd MOLD/BUCK CH7 .....42 D3
Dale Dr CHNE CH2 .....25 E1
Dale Rd CO CH5 .....19 H5
Daleside CHNE CH2 .....25 E1
  MOLD/BUCK CH7 .....42 A3
Dale St CHSE CH3 .....37 H5
Dalton Cl CH/BCN CH1 .....25 H1
Dane Cl CHSW/BR CH4 .....48 A2
Dane Gv CHNE CH2 .....27 E1
Daniell Wy CHSE CH3 .....37 G3
Daniel Owen Sq
  MOLD/BUCK CH7 * 40 C3
Darlington Crs CH/BCN CH1 .....10 D5
Darwin Rd CH/BCN CH1 .....23 F5
Daulwyn Rd MOLD/BUCK CH7 .....43 F1
Dauncey Cl CHNE CH2 .....12 D5
Dawn Cl CHSW/BR CH4 .....42 C4
Dawpool Cl CHNE CH2 .....25 E4
Dawson Dr CH/BCN CH1 .....36 D1
Daytona Dr MOLD/BUCK CH7 .....18 B5
Ddol Awel MOLD/BUCK CH7 .....40 A3
Deanery Cl CHNE CH2 .....24 D5
Dean's Av CO CH5 .....19 F2
Deansbury Cl FLINT CH6 .....4 B5
Deans Pl CO CH5 .....19 G2
Dee Banks CHSE CH3 .....37 H4
Dee Fords Av CHSE CH3 .....37 H3
Dee Hills Pk CHSE CH3 .....3 H4
Dee La CHSE CH3 .....3 H4
Dee Rd CHNE CH2 .....15 E5
  CO CH5 .....19 G3
  CO CH5 .....21 F2
Deeside Crs CH/BCN CH1 .....22 B4
Deeside La CH/BCN CH1 .....22 B4
Dee Vw CO CH5 .....20 B5
Dee View Rd CO CH5 .....19 F2
Deganwy Wy MOLD/BUCK CH7 .....30 D5
Degas Cl CO CH5 .....18 D1
Deiniol's Rd CO CH5 .....32 D2
Delamere Av MOLD/BUCK CH7 .....43 E4
Delamere St CH/BCN CH1 .....2 D2
The Dell CHSE CH3 .....27 E4
Delta Ct CHSW/BR CH4 .....47 E1
Delves Wk CHSE CH3 .....38 A5
Delvine Dr CHSW/BR CH4 .....48 B3
Demage La CH/BCN CH1 .....12 B3
Denbigh Cl CHNE CH2 .....25 E1
Denbigh Ct MOLD/BUCK CH7 .....30 D5
Denbigh Rd MOLD/BUCK CH7 .....40 B1
Denbigh St CH/BCN CH1 .....2 B1
Denford St CHSW/BR CH4 .....45 H3
Denhall Cl CHNE CH2 .....25 E4
Dennis Dr CH/BCN CH1 .....23 H4
Denstone Dr CHSW/BR CH4 .....48 B3
Dentith Dr CH/BCN CH1 .....23 H4
Derby Pl CHNE CH2 .....3 K5
Derwen Cl CO CH5 .....19 F1
Derwent Rd CHNE CH2 .....25 F2
Deva Av CHSW/BR CH4 .....47 G1
  CO CH5 .....19 E2
Deva Cl FLINT CH6 .....5 F4
Deva La CHNE CH2 .....24 D3

Deva Link CH/BCN CH1 .....36 B1
Deva Ter CHSE CH3 .....3 H4
Devon Cl CO CH5 .....19 E3
Devon Rd CHNE CH2 .....25 G4
Devonshire Pk CHSW/BR CH4 .....37 E5
Devonshire Rd CHSW/BR CH4 .....45 H5
Dicksons Dr CHNE CH2 .....25 E4
Dig La CO CH5 .....32 C4
Dinas Cl CH/BCN CH1 .....35 G1
Dinghouse Rd MOLD/BUCK CH7 .....31 F5
Dinghouse Wd
  MOLD/BUCK CH7 .....43 F1
Dingle Bank CHSW/BR CH4 .....38 D5
Dirty Mile CO CH5 .....43 H5
Disraeli Cl CO CH5 .....31 G4
Dock Rd CO CH5 .....19 F1
Dodd's Dr CO CH5 .....19 G2
Dol Awel CO CH5 .....31 G3
Dolphin Ct CHSW/BR CH4 .....36 B5
Donne Pl CH/BCN CH1 .....18 C1
Donnington Wy CHSW/BR CH4 .....36 A5
Dorchester Rd CHSW/BR CH4 .....48 A2
Dorfold Wy CHNE CH2 .....25 F3
Dormer Cl CHSE CH3 .....51 F2
Dorset Pl CHNE CH2 .....25 H1
Dorset Rd CHNE CH2 .....25 G2
Douglas Pl CHSW/BR CH4 .....47 H1
Dover Rd CHSW/BR CH4 .....48 B2
Dovey Cl CO CH5 .....19 E3
  CO CH5 .....31 G3
Downham Pl CH/BCN CH1 .....23 H5
Downsfield Rd MOLD/BUCK CH7 .....40 A3
Dreflan MOLD/BUCK CH7 .....40 B2
Drive A CO CH5 .....9 F4
Drive B CO CH5 .....9 F4
Drive C CO CH5 .....9 F5
Drive D CO CH5 .....9 F5
Drome Rd CO CH5 .....9 F5
Drury La CO CH5 .....9 F3
  MOLD/BUCK CH7 .....43 F2
Drury New Rd MOLD/BUCK CH7 .....43 F2
Dryden Cl CO CH5 .....31 F4
Duckers La CO CH5 .....32 D2
Duffryn Cl MOLD/BUCK CH7 .....43 E3
Duke's Field Dr
  MOLD/BUCK CH7 .....42 D2
Duke St CH/BCN CH1 .....2 E6
  FLINT CH6 .....4 D2
  MOLD/BUCK CH7 .....29 E3
Dukesway CHNE CH2 .....25 F2
Dulas Ct CHNE CH2 .....25 F2
Dulverton Av CHSE CH3 .....38 B2
Dunbar Cl CO CH5 .....7 E5
Dundas St CO CH5 .....20 C4
Dunham Wy CHNE CH2 .....25 G3
Dunlin Av CO CH5 .....19 H3
Durban Av CHSE CH3 .....38 C5
Dunham Cl CH/BCN CH1 .....24 A4
Dwyfor Av MOLD/BUCK CH7 .....41 G2
Dyfed Dr CO CH5 .....20 C5
Dylan Cl CO CH5 .....31 F5
Dyserth Rd CH/BCN CH1 .....35 G1

E

Eardswick Cl CHNE CH2 .....37 E1
Earle's Crs CO CH5 .....32 D1
Earl Road MOLD/BUCK CH7 .....40 C2
Earls Oak CHNE CH2 .....25 G2
Earls Port CH/BCN CH1 .....2 B3
Earlston Ct CHSE CH3 .....38 A1
Earl St FLINT CH6 .....4 D2
Earlsway CHSW/BR CH4 .....36 B5
East Cl MOLD/BUCK CH7 .....41 F3
Eastern Pathway
  CHSW/BR CH4 .....3 G7
Eastfields Gv CH/BCN CH1 .....22 D1
Eastgate Rw North CH/BCN CH1 .....2 E4
Eastgate Rw South CH/BCN CH1 .....2 E4
Eastgate St CH/BCN CH1 .....2 E4
East Gn CO CH5 .....21 F3
East Vw MOLD/BUCK CH7 .....29 F5
Eaton Av CHSW/BR CH4 .....37 E5
  CO CH5 .....19 G3
Eaton Cl CHSW/BR CH4 .....45 H3
Eaton Cv CHSW/BR CH4 .....47 H2
Eaton Ms CHSW/BR CH4 .....37 E5
Eaton Rd CHSW/BR CH4 .....37 E5
Ebury Pl CHSW/BR CH4 .....45 H3
Eccleston Av CHSW/BR CH4 .....49 E1
Echo Cl CHSW/BR CH4 .....47 H2
Edgar Pl CHSW/BR CH4 .....3 E5
Edge Gv CHNE CH2 .....3 K3
Edinburgh Wy CHSW/BR CH4 .....3 H6
Edmund St MOLD/BUCK CH7 .....40 C4
Edna St CHNE CH2 .....3 J1
Edwards Rd CHSW/BR CH4 .....48 B1
Edwin Dr FLINT CH6 .....5 E4
Egerton Dr CHNE CH2 .....25 E1
Egerton Rd CH/BCN CH1 .....25 G4
Egerton St CH/BCN CH1 .....2 E2
Eggbridge La CHSE CH3 .....51 F2
Eglwys Cl MOLD/BUCK CH7 .....42 B5
Eilder Dr CHNE CH2 .....47 H2
Elfed Dr MOLD/BUCK CH7 .....42 A5
Elgin Cl CHSE CH3 .....37 H1
Elidie Cl CO CH5 .....18 D1
Eliot Cl CO CH5 .....31 F4
Elizabeth Crs CHSW/BR CH4 .....3 H6
Ellesmere Av CHNE CH2 .....25 E4
  CO CH5 .....46 A3
Ellesmere Rd MOLD/BUCK CH7 .....41 H5
Elm Av CO CH5 .....19 E2
  FLINT CH6 .....4 C3
Elm Cft CO CH5 .....32 D2
Elm Dr MOLD/BUCK CH7 .....18 A5
  MOLD/BUCK CH7 .....40 B2
Elm Gv CHSW/BR CH4 .....47 H1
  MOLD/BUCK CH7 .....42 C4

Elm Rd CO CH5 .....31 H1
Elm Sq CHSW/BR CH4 .....48 A1
The Elms CO CH5 .....31 G5
Elm Wk MOLD/BUCK CH7 .....41 H2
Elm Wy CO CH5 .....31 F2
Elmwood Av CHNE CH2 .....25 G5
Elmwood Cl CO CH5 .....32 C5
Elstree Av CHSE CH3 .....38 A1
Elwy Cl MOLD/BUCK CH7 .....41 H2
Elwy Crs FLINT CH6 .....4 C5
Embassy Cl CH/BCN CH1 .....23 F4
Enderby Rd CH/BCN CH1 .....2 C1
Endsleigh Cl CHSE CH3 .....25 F1
Endsleigh Gdns CHNE CH2 .....25 F1
Englefield Crs CHSW/BR CH4 * 41 G2
Englefield Dr FLINT CH6 .....5 F4
  CO CH5 .....19 E2
Ennerdale CHNE CH2 .....25 G2
Ermine Rd CHNE CH2 .....25 F5
Erw Fach MOLD/BUCK CH7 .....41 G1
Erw Goed MOLD/BUCK CH7 .....41 G1
Essex Rd CHNE CH2 .....25 H4
Estuary Vw CO CH5 .....31 H2
Etheida Dr CHNE CH2 .....25 H2
Etna Rd MOLD/BUCK CH7 .....42 D1
Etterick Pk CHSE CH3 .....37 H2
Ettrick Pk CHSE CH3 .....37 H2
Eurgain Av CO CH5 .....18 D3
Evansleigh Dr CO CH5 .....33 F1
Evans St FLINT CH6 .....4 D2
Eversley Cl CHNE CH2 .....24 D5
Eversley Pk CHNE CH2 .....24 D5
Ewart St CHSW/BR CH4 .....35 E5
Ewloe Pl MOLD/BUCK CH7 .....42 C1
Exeter Pl CH/BCN CH1 .....24 A4
Exton Pl CO CH5 .....36 D1

F

Factory Rd CO CH5 .....21 H5
Fairfield Rd CO CH5 .....25 H5
  CHSW/BR CH4 .....45 G3
  CO CH5 .....20 C4
  MOLD/BUCK CH7 .....40 D3
Fairford Rd CHSW/BR CH4 .....48 A1
Fairholme Cl CH/BCN CH1 .....11 E5
Fairoaks Dr MOLD/BUCK CH7 .....18 D3
Fairway CO CH5 .....33 F1
Fairway Cl CO CH5 .....19 E4
Farbailey Cl CHSW/BR CH4 .....45 G3
Farfield Av CO CH5 .....19 F2
Farm Cl MOLD/BUCK CH7 .....42 C3
Farm Dr CO CH5 .....6 D5
Farmfield Cl CO CH5 .....20 A4
Farm Rd CO CH5 .....20 D2
  MOLD/BUCK CH7 .....42 C3
Farndon Cl CHSW/BR CH4 .....45 H3
Faulkners La CHSE CH3 .....38 C5
Faulkner St CHNE CH2 .....37 G1
Feathers La CH/BCN CH1 * 2 D5
Feathers St FLINT CH6 .....4 D2
Fedwen Arian CHSW/BR CH4 .....43 F3
Feilden Ct CH/BCN CH1 .....12 A5
Fern Cl FLINT CH6 .....4 C4
Fern Gv CO CH5 .....31 H1
Fernhill Rd CH/BCN CH1 .....23 H3
Fernside Rd CO CH5 .....19 H5
Ferry Bank CO CH5 .....20 D4
Ferry Ct CO CH5 .....21 F5
Ferry La CH/BCN CH1 .....35 F3
Ffawydden MOLD/BUCK CH7 .....42 C2
Fford Bryn Estyn
  MOLD/BUCK CH7 .....40 A3
Ffordd Argoed
  MOLD/BUCK CH7 .....41 E2
  MOLD/BUCK CH7 .....42 C2
Ffordd Brenig
  MOLD/BUCK CH7 .....41 H2
Ffordd Brigog
  MOLD/BUCK CH7 .....41 H2
Ffordd Cae Llwyn
  MOLD/BUCK CH7 .....18 D4
Ffordd Celyn MOLD/BUCK CH7 .....28 D2
Ffordd Cledwen CHSW/BR CH4 .....45 H2
Ffordd Dawel MOLD/BUCK CH7 .....28 D3
Ffordd Dol Goed
  MOLD/BUCK CH7 .....40 B4
Ffordd Edwin MOLD/BUCK CH7 .....16 D4
Ffordd Fer MOLD/BUCK CH7 .....41 G2
Ffordd Ffynnon CO CH5 .....31 G4
Ffordd Gelfft MOLD/BUCK CH7 .....18 D3
Ffordd Glyn MOLD/BUCK CH7 .....40 A4
Ffordd Glyndwr FLINT CH6 .....5 E4
  MOLD/BUCK CH7 .....16 D4
Ffordd Gwynedd
  MOLD/BUCK CH7 .....16 D4
Ffordd Hengoed
  MOLD/BUCK CH7 .....40 B4
Ffordd Las MOLD/BUCK CH7 .....29 E3
Ffordd Llanarth CO CH5 .....18 D2
Ffordd Llewelyn FLINT CH6 .....5 E1
Ffordd Mellion
  MOLD/BUCK CH7 .....18 D4
Ffordd Newydd
  MOLD/BUCK CH7 .....18 D5
  MOLD/BUCK CH7 .....40 A4
Ffordd Offa MOLD/BUCK CH7 .....41 G3
Ffordd Ogwen
  MOLD/BUCK CH7 .....41 H2
Fordd Owen MOLD/BUCK CH7 .....16 D3
Ffordd Pant Gwyn
  MOLD/BUCK CH7 .....18 D3
Ffordd Pel-y-Dryn CO CH5 .....31 H3
Ffordd Pennant
  MOLD/BUCK CH7 .....40 B1
Ffordd Pentre
  MOLD/BUCK CH7 .....40 D3
Ffordd Tegid CO CH5 .....31 F4

Ffordd Trem y Foel
  MOLD/BUCK CH7 .....40 B4
Ffordd y Fran FLINT CH6 .....5 E5
Ffordd y Goedwig
  MOLD/BUCK CH7 .....43 F5
Fford Eidon MOLD/BUCK CH7 .....29 E2
Fford Ganol MOLD/BUCK CH7 .....29 E3
Fford Tirion MOLD/BUCK CH7 .....29 E5
Fiddlers La CH/BCN CH1 .....11 E4
Field Cl FLINT CH6 .....4 C4
Field Farm La MOLD/BUCK CH7 .....42 B1
Field Farm Rd MOLD/BUCK CH7 .....42 B1
Fielding Cl CO CH5 .....31 F4
Field Pk CO CH5 .....18 D5
Fieldside CO CH5 .....32 B5
Field Vw CO CH5 .....32 D1
Fieldway CH/BCN CH1 .....10 D4
  CHNE CH2 .....25 F5
Fifth Av FLINT CH6 .....4 D4
Filkin's La CHSE CH3 .....37 H5
Finchett Dr CH/BCN CH1 .....2 A1
Firbeck Cl CHSW/BR CH4 .....45 H4
Fir-brook Av CO CH5 .....19 G2
Firs Cl MOLD/BUCK CH7 .....32 B2
First Av CO CH5 .....9 E5
  FLINT CH6 .....4 D4
The Firs MOLD/BUCK CH7 .....40 D4
Fir Tree Av CHSW/BR CH4 .....48 C2
Fir Tree La CHSE CH3 .....38 D5
Fishermans' Rd CO CH5 .....19 F1
Fisher Rd CH/BCN CH1 .....23 H5
Five Ashes Rd CHSW/BR CH4 .....48 C2
Flag La North CHNE CH2 .....25 F1
Flaxmere Dr CHSE CH3 .....38 A4
Flookersbrook CHNE CH2 .....37 F1
Florita Cl CO CH5 .....18 D1
Foregate St CH/BCN CH1 .....3 F4
Forest Dr CHSW/BR CH4 .....45 G4
Forest St CH/BCN CH1 .....3 G4
Forest Wk MOLD/BUCK CH7 .....43 F3
Forge Wy CHSW/BR CH4 .....48 A5
Fourth Av CO CH5 .....8 D4
  FLINT CH6 .....4 D4
Fowler Rd CH/BCN CH1 .....23 C5
Foxcote Cl CHSW/BR CH4 .....45 G4
Fox Cover CHSE CH3 .....27 E4
Fox Covert La CHSW/BR CH4 .....13 H4
  CHNE CH2 .....26 A1
Foxes Cl CO CH5 .....32 D1
Foxes Wk CHSE CH3 .....37 H5
Foxglove Cl CHSE CH3 .....51 G1
Fox La CHNE CH2 .....15 G2
Fox Lea CH/BCN CH1 .....22 D1
Fox's Dr CO CH5 .....24 D3
Foxwist Cl CHNE CH2 .....37 E1
Francis Cl CH/BCN CH1 .....3 G3
Francis St CH/BCN CH1 .....3 G2
Fraser Cl CHSW/BR CH4 .....48 B3
Fraser Dr MOLD/BUCK CH7 .....42 B3
Friars Ct CO CH5 .....32 B4
Frodsham Sq CH/BCN CH1 .....2 E3
Frodsham St CH/BCN CH1 .....2 E3
Fron Heulog CO CH5 .....31 G3
Fron Rd CO CH5 .....19 G3
Furne Rd CH/BCN CH1 .....23 H5

G

Gainford Av CO CH5 .....19 E2
Gala Cl CHSW/BR CH4 .....45 H4
Gardd Eirlys MOLD/BUCK CH7 .....41 H3
Gardd Eithin MOLD/BUCK CH7 .....18 B5
Gardd-y-Gwanwyn
  MOLD/BUCK CH7 * 18 B5
Garden Ct CH/BCN CH1 .....2 D3
Garden La CH/BCN CH1 .....2 C2
Garden Ter CHSE CH3 .....3 K3
Garden Wy CO CH5 .....19 H3
Garratt Cl CO CH5 .....18 C1
Garth Dr CHNE CH2 .....24 D4
Garth Ganol FLINT CH6 .....5 E5
Garthorpe Av CO CH5 .....19 F1
Garthorpe Cl CO CH5 .....19 F1
Gas La MOLD/BUCK CH7 .....29 E3
Gateheath Dr CHNE CH2 .....25 E2
Gawer Pk CH/BCN CH1 .....24 D5
Gaymoore Cl CHNE CH2 .....2 D1
Gayton Cl CHNE CH2 .....25 F4
Gelli Dywod MOLD/BUCK CH7 .....40 B4
George St CH/BCN CH1 .....2 E3
Gerrards Av CHSE CH3 .....37 H5
Gipsy La CH/BCN CH1 .....12 A4
Gladstone Av CH/BCN CH1 .....2 A3
Gladstone Rd CH/BCN CH1 .....2 B1
  CHSW/BR CH4 .....19 H3
Gladstone St CO CH5 .....19 H3
  CO CH5 .....40 C5
  MOLD/BUCK CH7 .....40 C5
Gladstone Ter CO CH5 .....33 E1
Gladstone Wy CO CH5 .....32 D3
Glamis Cl CHSE CH3 .....37 H2
Glan Aber MOLD/BUCK CH7 * 40 C3
Glan Aber Pk CHSW/BR CH4 .....36 B5
Glan Alun MOLD/BUCK CH7 .....40 C4
Glan Gors FLINT CH6 .....5 E5
Glanrafon Rd MOLD/BUCK CH7 .....40 D3
Glan y Fferi CO CH5 .....31 F3
Glan yr Eglwys
  MOLD/BUCK CH7 * 16 D3
Glasil Wyn CO CH5 .....31 F3
Glastonbury Av CHNE CH2 .....25 G2
Glebe Mdw CHNE CH2 .....15 E5
Gleggs Ct CHSE CH3 .....38 A5
Glendale Av CO CH5 .....33 E1
Gleneagles Cl CHSE CH3 .....38 A1
Glenesk Ct CO CH5 .....21 E3

Glenside Cl CH/BCN CH1 .....
The Glen CH/BCN CH1 .....
Globe Wy MOLD/BUCK CH7 .....
Gloucester Av CO CH5 .....
Gloucester St CH/BCN CH1 .....43 F5
Glovers Loom CHSE CH3 .....
Glynne Ct MOLD/BUCK CH7 * 40 C4
Glynnedale Pk CO CH5 .....
Glynne St CO CH5 .....
Glynne Wy CO CH5 .....
Glyn Teg MOLD/BUCK CH7 * .....
Glynteg MOLD/BUCK CH7 .....
Golftyn Dr CO CH5 .....
Golftyn La CO CH5 .....
  MOLD/BUCK CH7 .....
Gonsley Cl CHNE CH2 .....
Goodwood Cl CH/BCN CH1 .....
Goodwood Gv MOLD/BUCK CH7 .....
Gordon La CHNE CH2 .....
Gordon Ter MOLD/BUCK CH7 * .....
Cornel Av CO CH5 .....
Gorse Stacks CH/BCN CH1 .....
Gorse Wy CHSE CH3 .....
Gosforth Pl CHNE CH2 .....
Gosmore Rd MOLD/BUCK CH7 .....
Goss St CH/BCN CH1 .....
Gowy Rd CHNE CH2 .....
Goya Cl CO CH5 .....
Grafton Ms CHNE CH2 .....
Graham Rd CH/BCN CH1 .....
Granby Ct CO CH5 .....
Grange Rd CHNE CH2 .....
  CHSE CH3 .....
  CO CH5 .....
Grangeside CHNE CH2 .....
Granston Cl MOLD/BUCK CH7 .....
Grasmere Cl CO CH5 .....
Grasmere Crs MOLD/BUCK CH7 .....
Grasmere Rd CHNE CH2 .....
Grays Rd MOLD/BUCK CH7 .....
Greenacre Rd CHSW/BR CH4 .....
Greenbank CHSW/BR CH4 .....
Greenbank Dr FLINT CH6 .....
Greenbank Rd CHNE CH2 .....
  CO CH5 .....
Greenbank Vls FLINT CH6 * .....
Greenfield Crs CHNE CH2 .....
  CHSE CH3 .....
Greenfield La CHNE CH2 .....
Greenfield Rd CHSE CH3 .....
  CHSW/BR CH4 .....
Greenfields CHNE CH2 .....
Greenfields La CHSE CH3 .....
Greenhill Av CO CH5 .....
Green La CH/BCN CH1 .....
  CHNE CH2 .....
  CHSE CH3 .....
  CHSE CH3 .....
Green La East CO CH5 .....
Green La (West) CO CH5 .....
Green Mdw CO CH5 .....
Green Pk CO CH5 .....
Green Side MOLD/BUCK CH7 .....
Greensway CHSW/BR CH4 .....
The Green MOLD/BUCK CH7 .....
Greenville Av CO CH5 .....
Green Wy CH/BCN CH1 .....
Greenway St CHSW/BR CH4 .....
Greenwood Av CHSW/BR CH4 .....
Gresford Av CHSE CH3 .....
Grey Cl CO CH5 .....
Grey Friars CH/BCN CH1 .....
Greyhound Park Rd
  CH/BCN CH1 .....
Greystones Rd CHSE CH3 .....
Griffin Cl CH/BCN CH1 .....
Griffiths Ct CO CH5 .....
Grindley Bank CHNE CH2 .....
Groomscroft CO CH5 .....
Groomsdale La CO CH5 .....
Grosvenor Dr MOLD/BUCK CH7 .....
Grosvenor Park Rd CH/BCN CH1 .....
Grosvenor Park Ter CH/BCN CH1 .....
Grosvenor Pl CH/BCN CH1 .....
Grosvenor Prec CH/BCN CH1 .....
Grosvenor Rd CH/BCN CH1 .....
  CHSW/BR CH4 .....
Grosvenor St CH/BCN CH1 .....
  MOLD/BUCK CH7 .....
Grove Gdns CHSE CH3 .....
Grove Rd CH/BCN CH1 .....
The Groves CH/BCN CH1 .....
Grove St CH/BCN CH1 .....
Guilden Gn CHSE CH3 .....
Guilden Sutton La CHSE CH3 .....
Guildford Cl CHSW/BR CH4 .....
Guy La CHSE CH3 .....
Gwel y Mynydd
  MOLD/BUCK CH7 .....
Gwernaffield Rd
  MOLD/BUCK CH7 .....
Gwylan Av CO CH5 .....
Gwynedd Dr FLINT CH6 .....

H

Hadfield Cl CO CH5 .....
Hadrian Dr CH/BCN CH1 .....
Hafan Deg MOLD/BUCK CH7 .....
Hafod Cl CH/BCN CH1 .....
  CO CH5 .....
Hafod Pk CO CH5 .....

Merton Dr CHSW/BR CH4 .....48 B3
Meynell Pl CH/BCN CH1 .....28 B4
Middlecroft CHSE CH3 .....26 D4
Milborne Cl CHNE CH2 .....25 E5
Milford St MOLD/BUCK CH7 .....40 C2
Millais Cl CQ CH5 .....18 D1
Mill Cl CHNE CH2 .....25 E3
Mill Cft FLINT CH6 .....5 F4
Millers Cl CHSE CH3 .....51 F3
Mill La CHNE CH2 .....25 E4
  CQ CH5 .....19 H3
  MOLD/BUCK CH7 .....42 C2
Mill St CHSW/BR CH4 .....3 F7
Mill View Rd CQ CH5 .....19 H3
Millway CHSE CH3 .....51 G2
Milton Rd CH/BCN CH1 .....24 A3
Milton St CH/BCN CH1 .....3 F5
Min Awel FLINT CH6 .....5 E5
Minerva Av CH/BCN CH1 .....35 H5
Moel Fammau Rd
  MOLD/BUCK CH7 .....29 F5
Moel Garod MOLD/BUCK CH7 .....40 A3
  MOLD/BUCK CH7 .....40 A3
Moel Gron MOLD/BUCK CH7 .....41 G2
Moel Parc FLINT CH6 .....5 E5
Moel View Dr MOLD/BUCK CH7 .....18 A5
Moel View Rd
  MOLD/BUCK CH7 .....41 H3
  MOLD/BUCK CH7 .....42 C4
Moelwyn Cl MOLD/BUCK CH7 .....41 H1
Mold Rd CHSW/BR CH4 .....45 E4
  CQ CH5 .....19 F2
  CQ CH5 .....30 D3
  MOLD/BUCK CH7 .....30 A5
  MOLD/BUCK CH7 .....30 C3
  MOLD/BUCK CH7 .....41 F3
Moldsdale Rd MOLD/BUCK CH7 .....40 D3
Mold Wy CQ CH5 .....31 F2
Mollington Ct CH/BCN CH1 .....11 H5
Monet Cl CQ CH5 .....18 C5
Montrose Ct CHSW/BR CH4 .....36 A5
Monza Cl MOLD/BUCK CH7 .....18 C5
  MOLD/BUCK CH7 .....42 A3
Moor Cft MOLD/BUCK CH7 .....29 G5
Moorcroft Av CHSE CH3 .....38 A3
Moorcroft Crs CHSE CH3 .....26 B5
Moorefields MOLD/BUCK CH7 .....42 D3
Moorfield Cl CQ CH5 .....32 A1
Moorfield Rd CQ CH5 .....32 A2
Moorhouse Cl CHNE CH2 .....25 E4
Moor La CHSE CH3 .....51 F2
  CQ CH5 .....30 C5
Morgan Cl CH/BCN CH1 .....20 A4
Morley Av CQ CH5 .....19 F3
Morley Cl CHNE CH2 .....24 A1
Mornington Crs
  MOLD/BUCK CH7 .....43 F2
Mortlake Crs CHSE CH3 .....40 B5
Morton Rd CH/BCN CH1 .....23 H5
Moss Bank CHNE CH2 .....24 D5
Moss Gv CHSW/BR CH4 .....47 G1
Mossley Ct CQ CH5 .....32 B4
Moston Rd CHNE CH2 .....25 E1
Mostyn Pl CH/BCN CH1 .....23 H5
Mostyn St CQ CH5 .....19 H3
Mountain Vw CHSW/BR CH4 .....47 H1
Mountain View Av
  MOLD/BUCK CH7 .....41 H2
Mountain View Cl CQ CH5 * 19 E5
Mount Cl MOLD/BUCK CH7 .....41 G3
Mountfield Rd CQ CH5 .....32 A2
Mount Pl CHSE CH3 .....3 J5
Mount Pleasant CHSW/BR CH4 .....36 A5
Mount Pleasant Av FLINT CH6 .....4 D4
Mount Pleasant Rd
  MOLD/BUCK CH7 .....43 E1
The Mount CHSE CH3 .....3 K4
Mount Wy CHSE CH3 .....51 F3
Muirfield Rd MOLD/BUCK CH7 .....42 B2
Muir Rd CH/BCN CH1 .....35 H1
Myrica Gv CHNE CH2 .....38 A1
Myrtle Gv CHNE CH2 .....37 H1
Myrtle St MOLD/BUCK CH7 .....42 A2

N

Nant Derw MOLD/BUCK CH7 .....40 A3
Nant Garmon
  MOLD/BUCK CH7 .....40 B3
Nant Glyn MOLD/BUCK CH7 .....42 C4
Nant Mawr Crs
  MOLD/BUCK CH7 .....42 B3
Nant Mawr Rd
  MOLD/BUCK CH7 .....42 B3
Nant Rd CQ CH5 .....19 E1
Nant-y-Coed MOLD/BUCK CH7 .....40 B2
Naomi Cl CH/BCN CH1 .....23 G4
Napier Rd CHNE CH2 .....24 D1
Nefyn Cl CQ CH5 .....18 D2
Nelson St CH/BCN CH1 .....3 G2
  CQ CH5 .....20 A3
Neston Dr CHNE CH2 .....25 E2
Neville Dr CHSE CH3 .....38 A5
Neville Rd CHSE CH3 .....38 A3
Nevin Rd CH/BCN CH1 .....35 G1
New Brighton Rd
  MOLD/BUCK CH7 .....29 E3
Newbury Rd CHSW/BR CH4 .....40 B3
Newby Wk CQ CH5 .....18 D1
New Crane Bank
  CH/BCN CH1 .....2 B4
New Crane St CH/BCN CH1 .....2 C5
Newcroft CHSE CH3 .....10 D4
Newgate Rw CH/BCN CH1 * 2 E5
Newgate St CH/BCN CH1 * 2 E5
Newhall Ct CHNE CH2 .....25 F3
Newhall Rd CHNE CH2 .....25 F3
New Park Rd CQ CH5 .....19 H5
New Rd CQ CH5 .....44 A3

New Roskell Sq FLINT CH6 .....5 E2
Newry Ct CHNE CH2 .....25 E5
Newry Pk CHNE CH2 .....25 E5
Newry Pk East CHNE CH2 .....25 E5
New St CQ CH5 .....19 G2
  MOLD/BUCK CH7 .....40 B3
Newthorn Pl MOLD/BUCK CH7 .....42 C3
Newton Cl MOLD/BUCK CH7 .....18 A5
Newton Dr MOLD/BUCK CH7 .....43 G2
Newton Hall Dr CHNE CH2 .....25 E4
Newton La CHNE CH2 .....25 E4
Newton Park Vw CHNE CH2 .....25 E4
Newtown Cl CH/BCN CH1 .....3 F2
New Union St CQ CH5 .....19 E1
Nicholas Cl CH/BCN CH1 .....2 D5
Nicholas Ct CH/BCN CH1 .....2 D5
Nicholas Street Ms
  CH/BCN CH1 .....2 D5
Nick Olson Cl CHNE CH2 .....27 E1
Nield Ct CHNE CH2 .....25 E2
The Nook CHNE CH2 .....25 F5
  CHSE CH3 .....26 B5
  CHSW/BR CH4 .....47 H1
  CQ CH5 .....19 F1
Norfolk Rd CHNE CH2 .....25 F3
Norley Dr CHSE CH3 .....38 B3
Normanby Dr CQ CH5 .....19 E3
Normandy Rd CHNE CH2 .....12 D5
Norman St CQ CH5 .....20 A5
Norman Wy CH/BCN CH1 .....23 H4
Norris Rd CH/BCN CH1 .....23 H4
Northern Pathway
  CHSW/BR CH4 .....3 G7
Northgate Av CH/BCN CH1 .....2 D3
Northgate St CH/BCN CH1 .....2 D3
North Gn CQ CH5 .....21 F3
Northop Cl CQ CH5 .....19 E1
Northop Rd FLINT CH6 .....16 D1
  MOLD/BUCK CH7 .....28 D1
North Rd CQ CH5 .....7 G4
North St CHSE CH3 .....35 E5
  CHSW/BR CH4 .....20 A4
  CQ CH5 .....33 F1
Northway CHSW/BR CH4 .....36 B5
Norton Av CHSE CH3 .....47 G1
Norton Cl CHSE CH3 .....38 B2
Norwood Dr CHSW/BR CH4 .....48 A1
Nun's Rd CH/BCN CH1 .....2 C5

O

Oak Bank La CHNE CH2 .....26 B2
Oak Cl CQ CH5 .....19 E2
Oakdale Cl CHSW/BR CH4 .....45 G4
Oak Dr MOLD/BUCK CH7 .....42 C1
Oakenholt La FLINT CH6 .....6 A4
Oakfield Av CHNE CH2 .....25 F1
Oakfield Ct CHNE CH2 .....25 F1
Oakfield Rd CH/BCN CH1 .....23 F5
  CQ CH5 .....19 F1
  MOLD/BUCK CH7 .....42 D3
Oaklands CHSE CH3 .....27 E4
Oaklea Av CHNE CH2 .....25 G5
Oakley Rd CQ CH5 .....32 D2
Oakmere Dr CHSE CH3 .....38 A4
Oak Rd CHSW/BR CH4 .....48 A1
The Oaks Dr CHNE CH2 .....24 D2
The Oaks CQ CH5 .....31 G5
Oak Tree Cl CQ CH5 .....19 H5
  MOLD/BUCK CH7 .....42 D2
Oaktree Ct CHNE CH2 .....25 F1
Oakwood Cl MOLD/BUCK CH7 .....40 A1
Oakwood Vls CQ CH5 .....19 F3
Old Aston Hl CQ CH5 .....31 G2
Old Chester Rd CQ CH5 .....31 G2
Oldfield Crs CHSW/BR CH4 .....48 A2
Oldfield Dr CHSE CH3 .....38 A3
Old Hall Gdns CHNE CH2 .....37 F1
Old Hall Pk CHSE CH3 .....27 E4
Old Hall Pl CH/BCN CH1 * 2 D5
Old Hall Rd CQ CH5 .....31 H3
Old Liverpool Rd CQ CH5 .....31 F3
Old London Rd FLINT CH6 .....4 B2
Old Mold Rd CQ CH5 .....31 F2
Old Pearl La CHSE CH3 .....38 A3
Old Port Sq CH/BCN CH1 * 2 C5
Old Seals Wy CHSW/BR CH4 .....36 B2
Old Wrexham Rd
  CHSW/BR CH4 .....36 D5
Onslow Rd CH/BCN CH1 .....25 G5
Orchard Cl CHNE CH2 .....25 E4
  CQ CH5 .....32 C1
  MOLD/BUCK CH7 .....42 C3
Orchard Ct CHSE CH3 .....37 H3
Orchard Cft CHSE CH3 .....26 D4
The Orchards CQ CH5 .....18 D5
Orchard St CH/BCN CH1 .....3 G2
The Orchard CHSE CH3 .....37 H4
Orchard Wy MOLD/BUCK CH7 .....40 B1
Orchid Cl CHNE CH2 .....49 H1
Ormonde Rd CHNE CH2 .....24 D5
Ormonde St CH/BCN CH1 * 3 G2
Osbourne Ct CQ CH5 .....19 F1
Oulton Av CHSW/BR CH4 .....25 F3
Oulton Rd CH/BCN CH1 .....2 C5
Overdale Av CHSW/BR CH4 .....41 H3
Overlea Crs CQ CH5 .....32 B2
Overlea Dr CQ CH5 .....32 B2
Overleigh Cl CHSW/BR CH4 .....37 F5
Overleigh Dr MOLD/BUCK CH7 .....42 A1
Overleigh Rd CHSW/BR CH4 .....36 D5
Overleigh Ter CHSW/BR CH4 .....36 D5
Overton Cl MOLD/BUCK CH7 .....42 D3
Overwood Av CH/BCN CH1 .....23 H1
Overwood La CH/BCN CH1 .....23 H5
  CH/BCN CH1 .....23 H5
Owen Cl CH/BCN CH1 .....23 H5
Oxford Rd CHSW/BR CH4 .....48 A1

P

Padarn Cl CHSW/BR CH4 .....47 G2
Paddock Rd CHSW/BR CH4 .....49 F5
Paddock Rw CH/BCN CH1 * 2 E5
The Paddock CHSW/BR CH4 .....36 C5
  CQ CH5 .....32 C2
Padeswood Dr
  MOLD/BUCK CH7 .....43 F5
Padeswood Rd North
  MOLD/BUCK CH7 .....42 C3
Padeswood Rd South
  MOLD/BUCK CH7 .....42 C3
Palace Cl FLINT CH6 .....4 B3
Palatine Cl CH/BCN CH1 .....23 G5
Palgrave Cl CH/BCN CH1 .....24 B4
Palmerston Crs CQ CH5 .....31 G4
Palmerstone St CQ CH5 .....24 C5
Pant Glas MOLD/BUCK CH7 .....28 D3
Pant Isa MOLD/BUCK CH7 .....28 D3
Panton Pl CH/BCN CH1 .....3 K1
Panton Rd CHNE CH2 .....37 G1
Pant Ucha MOLD/BUCK CH7 .....28 D3
Pant y Fownog Dr
  MOLD/BUCK CH7 .....41 H3
The Parade CHSW/BR CH4 .....23 H4
Paradise CHSW/BR CH4 .....3 F7
Paradise La CQ CH5 .....31 G4
Parc Bryn Castell CQ CH5 .....18 D5
Parc Hendy MOLD/BUCK CH7 .....40 A3
Parc Issa MOLD/BUCK CH7 .....41 H1
Park Av CH/BCN CH1 .....10 D4
  CHSW/BR CH4 .....20 B3
  CQ CH5 .....32 C2
  FLINT CH6 .....4 D3
  MOLD/BUCK CH7 .....40 B2
  MOLD/BUCK CH7 .....41 H2
Park Dr CHSE CH3 .....26 D5
Park Dr South CHNE CH2 .....37 H1
Parkfield Rd CHSW/BR CH4 .....45 H4
Parkgate Rd CH/BCN CH1 .....24 D5
Park Gv CQ CH5 .....19 G3
Park House Ms
  MOLD/BUCK CH7 * 40 C3
Parkhouse Ms
  MOLD/BUCK CH7 * 40 C3
Park Rd MOLD/BUCK CH7 .....42 D2
Park Rd West CHSW/BR CH4 .....36 B5
Parkside MOLD/BUCK CH7 .....42 C2
Parkside Av CQ CH5 * 18 D3
The Parks CQ CH5 .....18 D3
Park St CH/BCN CH1 .....2 E5
The Park CHSE CH3 .....38 D4
  MOLD/BUCK CH7 .....40 B3
Park Vw MOLD/BUCK CH7 .....17 H4
  MOLD/BUCK CH7 .....42 D2
Park Wk CHNE CH2 .....25 E5
Park Wy CH/BCN CH1 .....10 D5
Parkway CQ CH5 .....8 D5
  MOLD/BUCK CH7 .....40 B3
Parsons La CHNE CH2 .....24 C2
Patten Cl CQ CH5 .....31 F4
Peach Fld CHSE CH3 .....38 A5
Pearl La CHSE CH3 .....38 A3
Pear Tree Cl CQ CH5 .....19 H5
Pear Tree Wy CHNE CH2 .....25 C4
Peckforton Wy CHNE CH2 .....25 F2
Peel Ter CH/BCN CH1 .....3 K1
Pemba Dr MOLD/BUCK CH7 .....42 D2
Pemberton Rd CH/BCN CH1 * 23 F2
Pembroke Cl CHSW/BR CH4 .....49 F1
  CQ CH5 .....20 C5
Pembry Ri CQ CH5 .....18 D1
Penfold Hey CHNE CH2 .....25 F2
Pengwladys Av CQ CH5 .....19 E4
Penlan Pl CQ CH5 .....32 B2
Penley Rd MOLD/BUCK CH7 .....42 D3
Penmon Cl CH/BCN CH1 .....35 G1
Pennant St CQ CH5 .....19 F2
Penny Bank Cl CHSW/BR CH4 .....45 E4
Penrhos Ct MOLD/BUCK CH7 .....18 D5
Pensby Av CHNE CH2 .....25 E4
Pentland Cl CHSE CH3 .....37 H2
Pentre Hl FLINT CH6 .....16 D1
Pentre La MOLD/BUCK CH7 .....30 B5
Pen-y-Bryn MOLD/BUCK CH7 .....28 D3
Pen-y-Coed Rd
  MOLD/BUCK CH7 .....43 F1
Pen-y-Garreg Cl
  MOLD/BUCK CH7 .....41 H2
Pen y Llan St CQ CH5 .....19 E1
Penymaes MOLD/BUCK CH7 .....41 G2
Pen y Maes MOLD/BUCK CH7 .....42 B3
Pen-y-Pentre MOLD/BUCK CH7 .....29 E3
Pepper St CH/BCN CH1 .....2 E5
  CHSE CH3 .....38 C4
Percival Cl CHNE CH2 .....24 D1
Percival Rd CHNE CH2 .....24 D1
Percy Rd CHSE CH3 .....37 E5
Philip St CQ CH5 .....33 F2
Phillips Rd CH/BCN CH1 .....35 G1
Philip St CQ CH5 .....33 G1
Phoenix St CQ CH5 .....33 F2
Pickering St CHNE CH2 .....3 H1
Pickmere Dr CHSE CH3 .....38 A4
Picton Gorse La CHNE CH2 .....26 A1
Pierce St CQ CH5 .....20 C4
Pierpoint Ct CH/BCN CH1 .....2 D5
Pine Crest FLINT CH6 * 4 D3
Pine Gdns CHNE CH2 .....24 D3
Pine Gv CHNE CH2 .....26 A5
  MOLD/BUCK CH7 .....41 H3
The Pines CQ CH5 .....31 G5
Pine Tree Cl CHSW/BR CH4 .....45 G4
Pinewood Av CQ CH5 .....19 H1
Pinewood Rd MOLD/BUCK CH7 .....43 G2
Pinfold Ct CHSW/BR CH4 .....49 F1
Pinfold La CHSW/BR CH4 .....37 F5

  CHSW/BR CH4 .....49 E1
  MOLD/BUCK CH7 .....30 B2
Pingot Cft CHSE CH3 .....38 A5
Pipers Cl CHNE CH2 .....26 A5
Pipers La CHNE CH2 .....26 A5
Pippins Cl CQ CH5 .....19 H4
Pitmans La CQ CH5 .....32 B3
Plas Newton La CHNE CH2 .....25 G3
Plemstall Cl CHNE CH2 .....27 E1
Plemstall La CHNE CH2 .....15 F5
Plemstall Wy CHNE CH2 .....15 F5
Plough La CHSE CH3 .....39 E5
  CQ CH5 .....20 A5
Plumley Cl CHSE CH3 .....38 B3
Plum Ter CH/BCN CH1 .....2 C2
Plymouth St CQ CH5 .....19 H3
Poplar Av CQ CH5 .....20 A5
Poplar Cl CQ CH5 .....19 F5
Poplar Gv CQ CH5 .....31 F2
Poplar Rd CHSW/BR CH4 .....48 A2
The Poplars CQ CH5 .....31 G5
Porters Cft CHSE CH3 .....27 E4
Potters Wy MOLD/BUCK CH7 .....42 B2
Powell Rd MOLD/BUCK CH7 .....42 B4
Powell's Orch CHSW/BR CH4 .....36 D5
Powey La CH/BCN CH1 .....11 E1
Powys Cl CQ CH5 .....20 C5
  MOLD/BUCK CH7 .....42 D1
Powys Ct CH/BCN CH1 .....23 H4
The Precinct Wy
  MOLD/BUCK CH7 .....42 C3
Pren Av MOLD/BUCK CH7 .....41 H3
Prenton Pl CHSW/BR CH4 .....37 F5
Prescot St CHNE CH2 .....3 J1
Pretoria St CHSW/BR CH4 .....37 E5
Primrose Cl CHSE CH3 .....49 H1
  MOLD/BUCK CH7 .....18 C5
Primrose St CQ CH5 .....19 F2
Prince of Wales Av FLINT CH6 .....4 D3
Princes Av CH/BCN CH1 .....3 H3
Princes Dr FLINT CH6 .....5 E5
Princess Av MOLD/BUCK CH7 .....42 A1
Princess St CH/BCN CH1 .....2 D4
Prince's St CQ CH5 .....19 F2
  FLINT CH6 * 5 E3
Prince William Av CQ CH5 .....33 C1
Prince William Ct CQ CH5 .....31 H3
Prince William Cdns CQ CH5 * 32 D2
Priors Ct CQ CH5 .....19 H5
Priory Cl CH/BCN CH1 .....24 D5
Priory Pl CH/BCN CH1 .....3 J1
Private Wk CHSE CH3 .....37 H4
Promised Land La CHSE CH3 .....50 D2
Prospect Cl CQ CH5 .....19 H5
Prosser Rd CHNE CH2 .....12 D5
Provan Wy CH/BCN CH1 .....23 G4
Pulford Rd CHSW/BR CH4 .....23 H4
Pwll Glas MOLD/BUCK CH7 .....40 B2
Pyecroft St CHSW/BR CH4 .....37 E5

Q

Quarry Cl MOLD/BUCK CH7 .....18 A5
Quarry La CHSE CH3 .....38 C5
  CQ CH5 .....20 D3
  MOLD/BUCK CH7 * 28 D3
Quay La CQ CH5 .....19 F1
Queen's Av CH/BCN CH1 .....3 H3
  CQ CH5 .....19 E1
  FLINT CH6 .....33 F1
  FLINT CH6 .....5 E4
Queensbury Dr FLINT CH6 .....4 B3
Queens Crs CHNE CH2 .....25 G3
Queen's Dr CHSW/BR CH4 .....3 H6
  MOLD/BUCK CH7 .....42 C3
Queen's La MOLD/BUCK CH7 .....40 D4
Queens Pk MOLD/BUCK CH7 .....40 A2
Queen's Park Rd CHSW/BR CH4 .....3 F7
Queen's Park Vw CHSW/BR CH4 .....3 F7
Queens Pl CH/BCN CH1 .....3 H3
Queen's Rd CH/BCN CH1 .....3 H2
  CHSE CH3 .....38 A2
  CQ CH5 .....21 E2
Queen St CH/BCN CH1 .....2 C5
  CQ CH5 .....20 C4
  FLINT CH6 .....5 E3
Queensway CQ CH5 .....19 H3
  CHNE CH2 .....25 G4
Queen's Wy CHSW/BR CH4 .....45 G3

R

Radford Cl CQ CH5 .....19 H2
Radnor Cl CQ CH5 .....20 C5
Radnor Dr CHSW/BR CH4 .....48 B2
Raewood Av CQ CH5 .....31 G4
Raikes La MOLD/BUCK CH7 .....23 G4
Rake La CHNE CH2 .....13 E1
  CHSE CH3 .....38 F4
  CQ CH5 .....33 E5
Rake Wy CH/BCN CH1 .....10 D5
Ramsden Ct CHSW/BR CH4 .....48 B2
Ranwonath Ct CHNE CH2 .....25 F2
Rawson Rd CH/BCN CH1 .....35 H1
Raymond St CH/BCN CH1 .....2 C3
Rectors La CQ CH5 .....21 E5
Rectory Cl FLINT CH6 .....4 D4
Rectory La CQ CH5 .....41 H3
Red Hall Av CQ CH5 .....19 G2
Redhill Rd CHSW/BR CH4 .....48 A1
Redland Cl CHSW/BR CH4 .....36 B5
Red Rd MOLD/BUCK CH7 .....42 C1
Redwood Cl CHSW/BR CH4 .....47 H1
Reece Cl CHNE CH2 .....26 D1

  CHSW/BR CH4 .....49 E1
  MOLD/BUCK CH7 .....30 B2
Reeves Rd CHSE CH3 .....38 C5
Regency Ct CHNE CH2 .....25 G3
Regents Cl CHSE CH3 .....38 B5
Reservoir Ter CHSE CH3 .....38 C5
Rhodfa Cilcain MOLD/BUCK CH7 .....28 A5
Rhodfa Eurgain CQ CH5 .....19 H4
Rhodfa Cer y Parc CQ CH5 * 19 H4
Rhodfa Mynydd
  MOLD/BUCK CH7 .....41 H1
Rhoswen FLINT CH6 .....5 E4
Rhuddlan Rd CH/BCN CH1 .....23 G5
Richards Cft CHSE CH3 .....51 F2
Richmond Cl CHSE CH3 .....38 B3
Richmond Crs CHSE CH3 .....38 B5
Richmond Rd CQ CH5 .....31 G4
The Ridgeway CQ CH5 .....20 A5
The Ridgeway
  MOLD/BUCK CH7 .....42 D1
The Ridings CH/BCN CH1 .....25 F5
Ring Rd CHSE CH3 .....38 D5
  CHSE CH3 .....39 E5
Ringway CHSE CH3 .....39 E5
River La CHSW/BR CH4 .....37 E5
  CHSW/BR CH4 .....45 E2
River Rd CQ CH5 .....33 E5
Riverside Pk CQ CH5 .....32 C5
Riversmead CHSE CH3 .....38 A5
River Vw CQ CH5 .....20 C5
Robin Hood La
  MOLD/BUCK CH7 .....42 C3
Robinsons Cft CHSE CH3 .....38 C5
Rockcliffe MOLD/BUCK CH7 .....42 B2
Rock Rd CQ CH5 .....3 J1
Roebourne Ri CH/BCN CH1 .....23 G4
Roman Dr CH/BCN CH1 .....23 G4
Roman Wy MOLD/BUCK CH7 .....42 B2
The Rookery CHSW/BR CH4 .....36 A5
Rosedene Cl CHSE CH3 .....38 A5
Rose La MOLD/BUCK CH7 .....40 B2
Rosemary Cl CHSW/BR CH4 .....45 E4
Rosewood Av CHNE CH2 .....25 F2
Rosewood Gv CH/BCN CH1 2 .....25 F2
  MOLD/BUCK CH7 .....42 D1
Rosslyn Cl CQ CH5 .....19 H5
Rosslyn Rd CHSE CH3 .....38 C5
Rothesay Rd CHSW/BR CH4 .....48 B2
Round Hill Meadow CHSE CH3 .....38 A5
Rowan Cl CQ CH5 .....19 H5
Rowan Pk CHSE CH3 .....38 A5
Rowan Pl CHNE CH2 .....25 E2
Rowan Rd MOLD/BUCK CH7 .....42 C1
The Rowans CHSW/BR CH4 .....36 A5
Rowcliffe Av CHSW/BR CH4 .....48 A2
Rowden Crs CQ CH5 .....31 G4
Rowden St CQ CH5 .....20 C5
Rowley's Dr CQ CH5 .....19 H5
Rowton Bridge Rd CHSE CH3 .....38 A5
Rowton La CHSE CH3 .....38 A5
Royal Dr FLINT CH6 .....5 E4
Rufus Court Rw CH/BCN CH1 * 2 D4
Rumney Cl MOLD/BUCK CH7 .....42 D1
Rushfield Rd CHSW/BR CH4 .....48 A2
Rushton Dr CHNE CH2 .....25 F2
Russell St CHSE CH3 .....3 H5
Ruthin Cl MOLD/BUCK CH7 .....42 D1
Ruthin Rd MOLD/BUCK CH7 .....42 D1
Rutland Ct CQ CH5 .....20 C5
Rutland Pl CHNE CH2 .....25 G3
Rydal Cl MOLD/BUCK CH7 .....42 C1
Rydal Gv CHSW/BR CH4 .....48 B2
Ryeland St CQ CH5 .....20 C5

S

Saighton La CHSE CH3 .....51 H1
St Andrew's Dr
  MOLD/BUCK CH7 .....42 B2
St Annes Cl CHSE CH3 .....38 A5
St Anne St CH/BCN CH1 .....3 G2
St Bartholomews Ct CQ CH5 .....33 E5
St Catherine's Cl FLINT CH6 .....4 B3
St Chad's Rd CHNE CH2 .....24 C2
St Christophers Ct CHNE CH2 .....25 F2
St Davids Cl FLINT CH6 .....4 B3
  CQ CH5 .....33 E5
St David's Dr CQ CH5 .....33 E5
St David's La MOLD/BUCK CH7 .....42 D1
St David's Ter CHSW/BR CH4 .....3 F7
St Ethelwold's St CQ CH5 .....33 F1
St Georges CH/BCN CH1 * 2 D4
St George's Crs CHSE CH3 .....38 A5
  CHSW/BR CH4 .....37 E5
St Ives Wy CQ CH5 .....32 B4
St James Av CHNE CH2 .....25 F2
St James Ct CQ CH5 .....33 E5
St James St CH/BCN CH1 .....2 C3
St John's Rear Rd CHSW/BR CH4 .....3 J5
St John's Rd CHSW/BR CH4 .....3 J5
St John's St CH/BCN CH1 .....3 H4
St Mark's Av CQ CH5 .....33 E5
St Marks Rd CHSW/BR CH4 .....48 A2
St Martin's Wy CH/BCN CH1 .....2 C4
St Mary's Dr MOLD/BUCK CH7 .....41 H2
St Mary's Hl CH/BCN CH1 .....2 D5
St Mary's Ms MOLD/BUCK CH7 .....42 C2
St Mary's Wy CQ CH5 .....33 E5
St Mellor's Rd MOLD/BUCK CH7 .....41 H2
St Michaels Cl CHNE CH2 .....26 D1
St Michaels Rw CH/BCN CH1 * 2 D4
St Michaels Sq CH/BCN CH1 * 2 D5
St Olave St CH/BCN CH1 .....2 D5
St Oswalds Ct CH/BCN CH1 .....2 C3
St Oswalds Wy CH/BCN CH1 .....2 D3
St Peter's Pk MOLD/BUCK CH7 .....42 C2
St Peters Wy CHNE CH2 .....24 C2
St Thomas Pathway
  CH/BCN CH1 .....

...urgh St CH/BCN CH1 ....2 E4
...ry Av CHSW/BR CH4 ....47 G1
...La CHNE CH2 ....36 C1
...H5 ....20 A3
...Leap CHSW/BR CH4 ....1 F6
...La CHNE CH2 ....26 B1
...Ferry Rd CHSW/BR CH4 ....35 E5
...ry St FLINT CH6 ....5 E2
...St CH/BCN CH1 ....3 G2
...gh CHNE CH2 ....25 F5
...rd CO CH5 ....19 H5
...n Ter CHNE CH2 ....3 J4
...ter Ct CHSW/BR CH4 ....48 C5
...gham Av CHSE CH3 ....37 H2
...CHSE CH3 ....38 D5
...ood Av CHSW/BR CH4 ....45 G4
...rove MOLD/BUCK CH7 ....40 B4
...a CHSE CH3 ....37 H4
...CHSE CH3 ....50 B4
...V/BR CH4 ....47 G1
....21 E2
...Wy CO CH5 ....18 D3
...ll Hey CH/BCN CH1 ....10 D5
...d Rd CH/BCN CH1 ....23 H5
...La CHNE CH2 ....23 H5
...CHNE CH2 ....26 D1
...st CHNE CH2 ....37 F1
...d CO CH5 ....22 C1
...A CO CH5 ....21 E2
...1 Rd CH/BCN CH1 ....35 H2
...H5 ....21 C2
...aite Wy CO CH5 ....18 D3
...s St CHSE CH3 ....3 H3
...Av MOLD/BUCK CH7 ....18 C5
...Av CO CH5 ....9 E3
...H5 ....4 D4
...ield Rd CH/BCN CH1 ....2 A2
...Cl CHSE CH3 ....49 H3
...La CHNE CH2 ....25 H5
...Dr CHSW/BR CH4 ....36 B5
...Rd CHSW/BR CH4 ....36 B5
...t CH/BCN CH1 ....3 G3
...Cl MOLD/BUCK CH7 ....42 B2
...tone Rd CH/BCN CH1 ....23 H4
...CH/BCN CH1
...La CO CH5 ....44 A3
...pentine CHSW/BR CH4 ....36 C5
...sbury Av CHSE CH3 ....38 A2
...Dr FLINT CH6 ....4 B3
...peare Av CO CH5 ....31 F5
...n Cl CHSW/BR CH4 ....45 G4
...ton Av CHNE CH2 ....25 G5
...CO CH5 ....31 F4
...CHSE CH3 ....37 H2
...n Av CHSE CH3 ....38 A2
...Cl CO CH5 ....31 F4
...rd's La CHNE CH2 ....25 E4
...on Rd CHSE CH3 ....51 G2
...urne Av CHSW/BR CH4 ....48 C2
...on Av CHSW/BR CH4 ....31 F4
...gham Cl CH/BCN CH1 ....47 H3
...ook Rd CHNE CH2 ....23 H4
...tone St CH/BCN CH1 ....2 E6
...Rd CHNE CH2 ....40 C2
...ach Rd CHNE CH2 ....25 F3
...n La CO CH5 ....20 A4
...ck La CH/BCN CH1 ....9 G2
...ck Rd CO CH5 ....8 D2
...sbury Wy CHSW/BR CH4 ....48 A1
...ct CHNE CH2 ....3 G2
...y Cl CHSW/BR CH4 ....45 H3
...Ct CHNE CH2 ....4 K2
...rch Cft CHSW/BR CH4 ....45 G4
...ale Av MOLD/BUCK CH7 ....43 G1
...one Dr MOLD/BUCK CH7 ....42 A3
...stone Rd CHSW/BR CH4 ....46 A3
...on Cl CHNE CH2 ....12 D5
...n CHNE CH2 ....24 D1
...on Wy CHSW/BR CH4 ....48 A1
...T CH6 ....4 D4
...CHSE CH3 ....38 D5
...a CO CH5 ....44 A2
...r CH/BCN CH1
...La MOLD/BUCK CH7 ....18 A4
...D/BUCK CH7 ....30 D3
...n Pathway CHSW/BR CH4 ....48 A3
...on Av CO CH5 ....19 E2
...CH5 ....41 H1
...on Crs CHNE CH2 ....48 B2
...ford Rd CHSW/BR CH4 ....25 G4
...set St CHNE CH2 ....2 E1
...Cl CHSE CH3 ....49 H1
...on Av CHNE CH2 ....3 G1
...Bank CH/BCN CH1 ....24 D5
...H5 ....20 A5

Crescent Rd
...W/BR CH4 ....3 G6
Fields Cl
...Cl MOLD/BUCK CH7 ....42 B2
...on CO CH5 ....21 F3
...Cl MOLD/BUCK CH7 ....42 B2
...St CHSE CH3 ....37 H3
...Vw CHSW/BR CH4 ....37 G5
...D/BUCK CH7 ....42 D4
...View Rd CH/BCN CH1 ....2 B3
...aign Wy CH/BCN CH1 ....35 H2
...s Cl CHSE CH3 ....38 A5
...well Cl CHSE CH3 ....49 H1
...er Cl CO CH5 ....31 F5
...Wk CHSE CH3 ....3 K4
...on MOLD/BUCK CH7 ....43 G4
...n CO CH5 ....31 H3
...field Cl CO CH5 ....18 D3

FLINT CH6 ....4 C4
Springfield Dr CHNE CH2 ....25 F5
...MOLD/BUCK CH7 ....42 A3
Springfields CHNE CH2 ....26 D1
Spring St CO CH5 ....19 H2
Springwood Cl CH/BCN CH1 ....23 F5
The Square CHSE CH3 ....38 D4
Stadium Wy CH/BCN CH1 ....36 C1
Stafford Rd CO CH5 ....21 E2
Stainton Gv CO CH5 ....18 D1
Stamford La CHSE CH3 ....39 F4
Stamford Rd CHNE CH2 ....23 H5
Stamford Wy MOLD/BUCK CH7 ....43 G1
Standard Rd MOLD/BUCK CH7 ....31 E5
Stanley Est MOLD/BUCK CH7 ....42 B3
Stanley Park Ct CHSW/BR CH4 * 47 H2
Stanley Park Dr CHSW/BR CH4 ....47 H2
Stanley Pl CHNE CH2 ....3 C4
...CO CH5 ....19 H4
Stanley Place Ms CH/BCN CH1 * 2 C5
Stanley St CHNE CH2 ....3 H2
...MOLD/BUCK CH7 ....42 B3
Stanton Dr CHNE CH2 ....25 E4
Stankey La MOLD/BUCK CH7 ....17 E1
Station La CHNE CH2 ....27 E1
...CO CH5 ....32 B4
Station Rd CH/BCN CH1 ....3 H5
...CH/BCN CH1
...CO CH5 ....19 G5
...CO CH5 ....33 F2
Station Vw CHNE CH2 ....3 J3
Steam Mill St CHSE CH3 ....3 H5
Stearns Cl CH/BCN CH1 ....24 B4
Steele St CO CH5 ....19 G3
Stendall Rd CH/BCN CH1 ....36 B2
Stephen Gray Rd
...MOLD/BUCK CH7 ....41 E5
Steven Ct CHSE CH3 ....3 H3
Stile End CHNE CH2 ....27 E1
Stirling Cl CHSE CH3 ....37 H3
Stocks Av CHSE CH3 ....37 H4
Stocks La CHSE CH3 ....37 H3
Stone Cft CHSE CH3 ....38 A4
Stoneleigh Cl CO CH5 ....21 E3
Stone Pl CHNE CH2 ....37 C1
Stratford Rd CH/BCN CH1 ....23 H5
Strawberry Flds CHSE CH3 ....37 H3
Strawberry La CH/BCN CH1 ....11 F1
The Street CHNE CH2 ....14 D5
Strickland St CO CH5 ....20 A4
Stroyd-y-Nant
Stryd Henardd
...MOLD/BUCK CH7 ....40 C3
Stryd-y-Capel
...MOLD/BUCK CH7 ....40 C3
Stuart Cl CHSE CH3 ....38 B1
Stuart Pl CH/BCN CH1 ....3 F2
Stubbs Pl CHNE CH2 ....35 H1
Summerdale Rd CO CH5 ....19 H5
Summerfield Cl CHSW/BR CH4 ....45 F4
Summerfield Rd CHSE CH3 ....27 E4
Summersville Cl CHNE CH2 ....19 E2
Sumner Rd CH/BCN CH1 ....23 H5
Sumpter Pathway CHNE CH2 ....37 G1
Sunbury Crs CHSW/BR CH4 ....48 A1
Sunningdale MOLD/BUCK CH7 ....42 B1
Sunny Rdg MOLD/BUCK CH7 ....40 B1
Sunnyside CO CH5 ....32 C2
Surrey Rd CHNE CH2 ....25 G5
Sussex Rd CHNE CH2 ....25 G5
Sutherland Wy CHSE CH3 ....38 A1
Sutton Cl CHNE CH2 ....27 E1
...CO CH5 ....18 D3
Sutton Dr CHNE CH2 ....25 F4
Swain Av MOLD/BUCK CH7 ....43 E4
Swinchiard La FLINT CH6 ....4 D3
Swinchiard Wk FLINT CH6 ....4 D3
Swinleys Hey CHSE CH3 ....37 H5
Swn-y-Gwynt FLINT CH6 ....5 E5
Swn y Nant MOLD/BUCK CH7 * 40 C4
Swn-y-Nant MOLD/BUCK CH7 ....40 C4
Sycamore Av CO CH5 ....19 F2
Sycamore Cl CO CH5 ....31 G5
Sycamore Dr CHSW/BR CH4 ....48 A3
Sycamore Gv CHSW/BR CH4 ....45 G4
Sydney Rd CHNE CH2 ....2 B1
Sydney Wk FLINT CH6 ....4 D2

Third Av CO CH5 ....9 E5
...FLINT CH6 ....4 D4
Thirlmere Rd CHNE CH2 ....25 H4
Thomas Av CO CH5 ....31 F4
Thomas Brassey Cl CHNE CH2 ....3 G3
Thomas Cl CH/BCN CH1 ....24 A3
...CHNE CH2 ....27 E1
Thomas St FLINT CH6 ....4 D2
Thornberry Cl CHNE CH2 ....23 E1
Thornfield Av CO CH5 ....19 G5
Thornfields CO CH5 ....19 G5
Thornhill Cl CHSW/BR CH4 ....45 E4
Thornton Dr CHNE CH2 ....25 E4
Threos Cl MOLD/BUCK CH7 ....18 D5
Thurston Rd CHNE CH2 ....47 H2
Tilers Cl MOLD/BUCK CH7 ....42 B2
Timberfields Rd CH/BCN CH1 ....47 H2
Tir Afon MOLD/BUCK CH7 ....25 G3
Tir Wat MOLD/BUCK CH7 ....41 H3
Titian Cl CO CH5 ....18 D1
Tivaton Cl CO CH5 ....19 E3
Tiverton Cl CHNE CH2 ....25 F4
Toft Cl CHSW/BR CH4 ....48 B1
Toll Bar Rd CHSE CH3 ....38 B5
Tollemache Ter CHNE CH2 ....3 K3
Tomkinson St CHNE CH2 ....3 H1
Toogood Cl CHNE CH2 ....27 E1
Totland Gv CHNE CH2 ....25 F5
Towergate CH/BCN CH1 ....2 B4
Tower Rd CH/BCN CH1 ....2 B3
Townfield La CH/BCN CH1 ....24 A1
Trafford Av CHSE CH3 ....38 A5
Tram La MOLD/BUCK CH7 ....42 D2
Tram Rd MOLD/BUCK CH7 ....42 D1
Treborth Rd CH/BCN CH1 ....24 D5
Trefoil Cl CHSE CH3 ....50 A1
Tregele Cl CHNE CH2 ....35 G1
Trelawny Av FLINT CH6 ....5 F4
Trelawny Sq FLINT CH6 ....5 F4
Trelech MOLD/BUCK CH7 ....18 D5
Trem Afon MOLD/BUCK CH7 ....41 G2
Trem-y-Foel MOLD/BUCK CH7 ....28 D4
Trinity St CH/BCN CH1 ....2 D4
Trueman's St CO CH5 ....32 B4
Trueman's Wy CO CH5 ....32 B3
Tudor Av FLINT CH6 ....5 G4
Tudor Cl CO CH5 ....20 A4
...MOLD/BUCK CH7 ....18 A5
Tudor Wy CHSE CH3 ....37 H5
Tuscan Wy CO CH5 ....19 F1
Tushingham Cl CHSE CH3 ....38 A5
Twain Cl CO CH5 ....31 F4
Tyddyn St MOLD/BUCK CH7 ....40 C3

U

Ullswater Crs CHNE CH2 ....25 H3
Ullswater Rd MOLD/BUCK CH7 ....42 D1
Union Cl CH/BCN CH1 ....3 G4
Union Ter CH/BCN CH1 ....3 F3
Uplands Av CO CH5 ....19 E4
Upper Aston Hall La CO CH5 ....32 A5
Upper Bryn Coch
...MOLD/BUCK CH7 ....40 A4
Upper Bryn Rd CO CH5 ....19 E1
Upper Cambrian Rd
....2 B2
Upper Northgate St
...CH/BCN CH1 ....2 D1
Upton Cl CHNE CH2 ....24 D3
Upton La CHNE CH2 ....24 D2
Upton Pk CHNE CH2 ....25 E3
Uwch-y-Nant MOLD/BUCK CH7 ....41 G2

V

Vale Av MOLD/BUCK CH7 ....31 F5
Vale Cl CHSW/BR CH4 ....45 H4
Valley Dr CHNE CH2 ....25 F4
Vaughans La CHSE CH3 ....37 H4
Vaughan Wy CO CH5 ....19 E5
Venable's Rd CH/BCN CH1 ....24 A5
Vermeer Cl CO CH5 ....18 D1
Vernon Cl CHNE CH2 ....22 D1
Vernon Rd CH/BCN CH1 ....3 F4
The Vetches CHSE CH3 ....27 E4
Vicarage Cl CHSE CH3 ....27 E4
Vicarage Rd CHNE CH2 ....37 G1
Vicars Cross Rd CHSE CH3 ....38 A2
Vicar's La CH/BCN CH1 ....3 F5
Vickers Cl CO CH5 ....32 B1
Victoria Av MOLD/BUCK CH7 ....42 D2
Victoria Cl CO CH5 ....36 D1
Victoria Crs CHSW/BR CH4 ....3 G6
...CO CH5 ....19 H3
Victoria Pathway
...CHNE CH2 ....3 G7
Victoria Rd CH/BCN CH1 ....3 G7
...CO CH5 ....36 D1
...CHSW/BR CH4 ....47 G1
...CO CH5 ....19 H3
...MOLD/BUCK CH7 ....42 B3
...MOLD/BUCK CH7 ....40 C2
Victoria St MOLD/BUCK CH7 ....40 D2
Victory Cl MOLD/BUCK CH7 ....42 A3
Viking Wy CO CH5 ....18 D1
Village Rd CHSE CH3 ....51 G5
...CHSE CH3 ....51 G5
Villa Rd CO CH5 ....21 G5
Vincent Dr CHSW/BR CH4 ....48 G1
Virginia Dr CH/BCN CH1 ....23 H4
Volunteer St CH/BCN CH1 ....2 E5
Vownog MOLD/BUCK CH7 ....28 D2

Vownog Newydd
...MOLD/BUCK CH7 ....29 E2
Vyrnwy Rd CHSW/BR CH4 ....47 G1

W

Walker St CHNE CH2 ....3 H1
Walls Av CH/BCN CH1 ....24 D5
Walnut Cl CHNE CH2 ....25 E2
Walpole Av CO CH5 ....31 H4
Walpole St CH/BCN CH1 ....2 C1
Walter St CH/BCN CH1 ....3 F1
Waltham Pl CHSW/BR CH4 * 48 B1
Walton Pl CH/BCN CH1 ....23 H5
The Waltons CHSW/BR CH4 ....49 F1
Wards Ter CHNE CH2 ....3 J1
Wared Dr MOLD/BUCK CH7 ....18 A5
Warkick Rd CH/BCN CH1 ....24 A4
Warren Crs MOLD/BUCK CH7 ....43 G3
Warren Dr CHSW/BR CH4 ....45 F4
Warrington Rd CHNE CH2 ....15 E5
...CHNE CH2 ....26 A4
Washington Dr CO CH5 ....31 H3
Watergate Rw North
...CH/BCN CH1 ....2 D4
Watergate Rw South
....2 D5
Watergate Sq CH/BCN CH1 ....2 D5
Watergate St CH/BCN CH1 ....2 D5
Waterloo Rd CHNE CH2 ....24 D5
Waters Edge CH/BCN CH1 ....2 B5
Waterside Vw CHNE CH2 ....2 E5
Waters Reams CHSE CH3 ....38 A4
Water St MOLD/BUCK CH7 ....40 C3
Water Tower St CH/BCN CH1 ....2 C3
Watertower Vw CHNE CH2 ....3 K3
Waterway CHSE CH3 ....51 G2
Watkin St CO CH5 ....33 F1
Watling Crs CHSW/BR CH4 ....37 F5
Wats Dyke Av
...MOLD/BUCK CH7 ....41 G2
Wat's Dyke Wy
...MOLD/BUCK CH7 ....29 E2
Watson's Cl CHSW/BR CH4 ....45 H4
Watts Cl MOLD/BUCK CH7 ....42 A3
Wavells Wy CHSE CH3 ....50 A2
Waverley Ter CHNE CH2 ....37 F1
Waverton Mill Quays
...CHSE CH3 ....51 G2
Wavertree Rd CHNE CH2 ....23 F4
Wayside Ct CHNE CH2 ....27 E1
Wealstone Ct CHNE CH2 ....25 F4
Weal Stone La CHNE CH2 ....25 F4
Weaver Gv CHNE CH2 ....15 E5
Weaver St CH/BCN CH1 ....2 D5
Webster Cl CHSW/BR CH4 ....45 H4
Wedgwood Rd CO CH5 * 32 A1
Weighbridge Rd CO CH5 ....8 A1
Welland Dr CO CH5 ....19 E2
Wellington Cl CO CH5 ....31 H4
Wellington Pl CH/BCN CH1 ....2 D1
Wellington Rd CHSW/BR CH4 ....45 G4
Wellington St CO CH5 ....20 A3
Well La CH/BCN CH1 ....12 A5
...CHNE CH2 ....25 F4
Wells Cl CHNE CH2 ....27 E1
Well St MOLD/BUCK CH7 ....42 A4
Welsh Rd CO CH5 ....20 D3
Wemyss Rd CH/BCN CH1 ....23 G5
Wenlock Crs CO CH5 ....32 D1
Wenlock Wy CHSW/BR CH4 ....48 A1
Wentworth Cl MOLD/BUCK CH7 ....42 B1
Wepre Cl CO CH5 ....19 E4
Wepre Dr CO CH5 ....19 H2
Wepre Hall Crs CO CH5 ....19 F3
Wepre La CO CH5 ....19 G4
Wepre Pk CO CH5 ....19 G4
Wervin Rd CHNE CH2 ....13 G5
Wesley St CO CH5 ....19 G1
West Bank CH/BCN CH1 ....24 D5
West View Dr
...MOLD/BUCK CH7 ....41 F3
Westbourne Crs
....42 B3
Westbourne Rd CH/BCN CH1 ....24 B5
Westbrook Dr MOLD/BUCK CH7 ....42 D4
Westbury Dr MOLD/BUCK CH7 ....43 F3
Westbury Wy CHSW/BR CH4 ....48 A1
Western Ap CHNE CH2 ....25 F5
Western Av CH/BCN CH1 ....35 G1
Western Crs CO CH5 ....25 F5
Westfield Cl CHSW/BR CH4 ....3 C6
West Lorne St CH/BCN CH1 ....2 C2
Westminster Av CHSW/BR CH4 ....48 C1
Westminster Ct CHNE CH2 ....3 J1
Westminster Crs CO CH5 ....20 B4
...CO CH5 ....48 C4
Westminster Ter CHNE CH2 ....36 D5
Weston Cl CO CH5 ....24 D4
Weston Gv CHNE CH2 ....25 F3
West St CHNE CH2 ....37 F1
West Vw MOLD/BUCK CH7 ....40 C3
....42 D4

White Oaks Dr MOLD/BUCK CH7 ..18 B5
Whites Meadow CHSE CH3 ....37 H5
White Way Cv CO CH5 * 21 E3
Whittle Cl CO CH5 ....53 F1
Whitton Dr CHNE CH2 ....25 F4
Wicker La CHSE CH3 ....27 F5
The Wiend CHNE CH2 ....25 E5
The Wigdale CO CH5 ....32 B4
Willan Rd CH/BCN CH1 ....23 C5
William Cl CHNE CH2 ....24 D5
William St CHNE CH2 ....3 J1
Willoway Rd CHSE CH3 ....38 A2
Willow Cl CHNE CH2 ....25 E1
...MOLD/BUCK CH7 ....43 F3
Willow Crs CHNE CH2 ....25 H5
....19 E2
...CO CH5 ....31 G4
Willow Dr CH/BCN CH1 ....23 G4
...FLINT CH6 ....4 B4
Willow Gv CHSE CH3 ....26 A5
...MOLD/BUCK CH7 ....30 B5
Willowherb Cl CHSE CH3 ....49 H1
Willow La CO CH5 ....20 D5
Willow Lea CH/BCN CH1 ....12 A4
Willow Rd CHSW/BR CH4 ....48 A1
The Willow CHSE CH3 ....30 C5
Willows Cl CHSW/BR CH4 ....48 A3
Willow Sq CO CH5 ....32 C2
Winchester Sq CHSW/BR CH4 ....48 A3
Windermere Av CHNE CH2 ....25 H5
...CO CH5 ....19 G2
Windmill Cl MOLD/BUCK CH7 ....42 C2
Windmill Ri CHNE CH2 ....25 E2
Windmill Rd MOLD/BUCK CH7 ....42 C2
Windsor Av CO CH5 ....19 G5
....20 A3
Windsor Dr CHSW/BR CH4 ....45 F4
...FLINT CH6 ....4 B3
Windsor Rd CHNE CH2 ....48 A1
Winkwell Dr CHSW/BR CH4 ....48 B2
Winscombe Dr CHSE CH3 ....38 B2
Winsford Wy CH/BCN CH1 ....36 A2
Wirral Vw CO CH5 ....19 E2
....31 H3
Withy Cft CHSE CH3 ....38 A5
Wold Ct CO CH5 ....32 C4
Woodbank La CH/BCN CH1 ....10 A1
Woodbank Rd CO CH5 ....31 F5
Wood Cft CHSE CH3 ....27 E5
Woodcroft Rd
....43 F1
Woodfield Av FLINT CH6 ....5 E4
Woodfield Cl CHSW/BR CH4 ....19 F3
...CO CH5 ....19 F3
Woodfield Gv CHNE CH2 ....25 H3
Wood Gn MOLD/BUCK CH7 ....40 D3
Woodland Bnk CHNE CH2 ....15 E5
Woodland Ct FLINT CH6 ....5 E4
Woodland Dr CO CH5 * 19 H3
Woodland Dr FLINT CH6 ....4 C4
Woodland St CO CH5 ....31 H3
Woodlands Cl MOLD/BUCK CH7 ....42 D4
Woodlands Ct CO CH5 ....32 B4
Woodlands Cl CO CH5 ....25 F5
...CO CH5 ....31 G5
Woodlands La CHSE CH3 ....25 G5
Woodlands Rd CHSW/BR CH4 ....49 H1
...CHSW/BR CH4 ....36 B5
....40 D4
The Woodlands CO CH5 ....44 A3
Wood La CHSW/BR CH4 ....45 G3
...CO CH5 ....25 G2
Woodlea Av CHNE CH2 ....25 G2
Woodside Cl CO CH5 ....32 D1
Woodside Rd CH/BCN CH1 ....23 F4
Wood St CHSE CH3 ....33 F2
Wood Ville CO CH5 ....32 C2
Worcester Pl CH/BCN CH1 ....2 B4
Wordsworth Cl CO CH5 ....31 F4
Wordsworth Crs CH/BCN CH1 ....24 B4
Wordsworth Ms CH/BCN CH1 ....24 B4
Wordsworth Sq CH/BCN CH1 ....24 A4
Worsley Av CH/BCN CH1 ....22 D1
Wrekin Wy CHSW/BR CH4 ....48 B5
Wrexham Rd CHSW/BR CH4 ....48 B5
...MOLD/BUCK CH7 ....40 D4
Wrexham St MOLD/BUCK CH7 ....40 C3
Wroxham Cl CHNE CH2 ....2 E1
Wycliffe Ct CHNE CH2 ....37 H2
Wylfa Av MOLD/BUCK CH7 ....41 F2
Wyndham St CH/BCN CH1 ....23 F5
Wynnstay Rd CHSW/BR CH4 ....45 H3

Y

Yarrow Cl CHSW/BR CH4 ....45 H4
Y Cedrwydd MOLD/BUCK CH7 ....41 H2
Y Dolydd MOLD/BUCK CH7 ....40 B4
Yerburgh St CHNE CH2 ....25 E5
Yew Tree Cl CHNE CH2 ....25 H3
Y Glfach MOLD/BUCK CH7 ....40 C4
The Yonne CH/BCN CH1 ....2 C4
York Av CO CH5 ....9 E4
York Dr CHNE CH2 ....14 D5
...CHNE CH2 ....27 E1
York Rd CO CH5 ....19 E1
York St CH/BCN CH1 ....3 F5
Yowley Rd CO CH5 ....31 G2
Yr Ydlan MOLD/BUCK CH7 ....41 G1

Abbey Gate School
CHNE CH2 ....2 D1
Acorn Business Park
FLINT CH6 ....4 C2
Acresfield Primary School
CHNE CH2 ....25 G1
Alun School
MOLD/BUCK CH7 ....40 C4
Argoed High School
MOLD/BUCK CH7 ....41 H1
Ashmount Industrial Centre
FLINT CH6 ....4 D2
Beaufort Park Hotel
MOLD/BUCK CH7 ....29 F4
Belgrave Infant School
CHSW/BR CH4 ....48 C2
Belmont Infant School
CH/BCN CH1 ....42 B3
Bishop (Bluecoat) CE High
School *CHSE* CH3 ....37 H4
Blacon Clinic
CH/BCN CH1 ....23 H4
Blacon County High School
CH/BCN CH1 ....23 G5
Blacon Hall Junior School
CH/BCN CH1 ....23 H4
Blacon Infant School
CH/BCN CH1 ....23 H4
Blossoms Hotel
CH/BCN CH1 ....3 F4
The Borders Industrial Park
CHSW/BR CH4 ....35 F5
Boughton Health Centre
CHSE CH3 ....3 J3
Boughton Heath Primary
School *CHSE* CH3 ....38 A4
Boughton St Pauls Nursery
& Infants *CHSE* CH3 ....3 H3
Bridgegate
CH/BCN CH1 ....2 C4
Bromfield Industrial Estate
MOLD/BUCK CH7 ....40 D4
Broncoed Business Park
MOLD/BUCK CH7 ....40 D5
Brookside Hotel
CHNE CH2 ....25 E5
Broughton Industrial Estate
CHSW/BR CH4 ....46 C1
Broughton J&I School
CHSW/BR CH4 ....45 H3
Broughton Shopping Park
CHSW/BR CH4 ....46 B3
Brymau Four Trading Estate
CHSW/BR CH4 ....35 G5
Brymau One Trading Estate
CHSW/BR CH4 ....35 H5
Brymau Three Trading Estate
CHSW/BR CH4 ....35 H5
Brymau Two Trading Estate
CHSW/BR CH4 ....35 H5
Bryn Awel Hotel
MOLD/BUCK CH7 ....40 C2
Bryn Coch Primary School
MOLD/BUCK CH7 ....40 C3
Bryn Deva Primary School
CH/BCN CH1 ....19 E1
Bryn Gwalia Primary School
MOLD/BUCK CH7 ....40 B3
Buckley CC
MOLD/BUCK CH7 ....43 E3
Buckley Health Centre
MOLD/BUCK CH7 ....42 C3
Cambrian Business Park
MOLD/BUCK CH7 ....41 E5
Castle Park Industrial Estate
FLINT CH6 ....4 D1
The Castle
CH/BCN CH1 ....2 D7
Catheralls Industrial Estate
MOLD/BUCK CH7 ....30 C5
The Catholic High School
MOLD/BUCK CH7 ....49 E1
Chantry Court
CH/BCN CH1 ....35 H2
Cherry Grove Primary School
CHSE CH3 ....37 H3
Cheshire County Officers
Sports Club *CHNE* CH2 ...25 H3
The Cheshire Military Museum
CH/BCN CH1 ....2 D6
Chester & Ellesmere Port
Police HQ *CH/BCN* CH1 ...24 B4
Chesterbank Business Park
CHSW/BR CH4 ....35 G5
Chester Boughton Hall
Cricket Club *CHSE* CH3 ...38 A3
Chester Business Centre
CH/BCN CH1 ....3 F4
Chester Business Park
CHSW/BR CH4 ....48 D4
Chester Cathedral
CH/BCN CH1 ....2 E5
Chester City FC (Deva Stadium)
CH/BCN CH1 ....35 H3
Chester College of Higher
Education *CH/BCN* CH1 ...36 D1

Chester County Court
CH/BCN CH1 ....2 D4
Chester Court Hotel
CHNE CH2 ....25 G5
The Chester Crabwall Manor
Hotel *CH/BCN* CH1 ....23 H2
Chester Crematorium
CHNE CH2 ....24 B5
Chester Figure Clinic
CH/BCN CH1 ....2 E4
Chester Golf Club
CHSW/BR CH4 ....2 A6
The Chester Grosvenor &
Grosvenor Spa Hotel
CH/BCN CH1 ....2 E4
Chester Racecourse
CH/BCN CH1 ....2 B6
Chester Retail Park
CH/BCN CH1 ....36 B2
Chester RUFC
CHSE CH3 ....38 C2
Chester Toy Museum
CH/BCN CH1 ....2 E5
Chester Visitors Centre
CH/BCN CH1 ....3 F4
Chester Zoo
CHNE CH2 ....13 F5
Christleton County High
School *CHSE* CH3 ....38 D5
Christleton Primary School
CHSE CH3 ....38 C4
Christleton Sports Centre
CHSE CH3 ....39 E5
Christleton Sports Club
CHSE CH3 ....39 E3
City Walls Medical Centre
CH/BCN CH1 ....2 C4
The Clinic
CH/BCN CH1 ....31 H3
Connahs Quay Health Centre
CQ CH5 ....6 C5
Connahs Quay Sports Centre
CQ CH5 ....6 D5
Cornist Park County Primary
School *FLINT* CH6 ....4 B3
Countess of Chester Hospital
CHNE CH2 ....24 C4
County Civic Centre
MOLD/BUCK CH7 ....28 D5
Crown Courts
CH/BCN CH1 ....2 D6
The Curzon Hotel
CHSW/BR CH4 ....36 C5
Custom House Lane Primary
School *CQ* CH5 ....19 G2
Dee Banks Special School
CHSE CH3 ....37 H5
Dee Point County Primary
School *CH/BCN* CH1 ....35 G1
Dee Road Infant School
CQ CH5 ....19 G2
Deeside College
CQ CH5 ....6 C5
Deeside Community Hospital
CQ CH5 ....19 H5
Deeside Industrial Estate
CQ CH5 ....9 F5
Deeside Stadium
CQ CH5 ....6 B5
Delyn & Deeside Business
Centre *CQ* CH5 ....31 F3
Dene Hotel
CHNE CH2 ....25 G5
Deva Business Park
CQ CH5 ....21 F1
Deva Industrial Park
CQ CH5 ....21 E4
Deva Roman Experience
CH/BCN CH1 ....2 D5
De Vere St David's Park Hotel
MOLD/BUCK CH7 ....31 G3
Dobshill Hospital
MOLD/BUCK CH7 ....43 G4
Dorin Park Special School
CHNE CH2 ....25 E3
Drury Industrial Estate
MOLD/BUCK CH7 ....43 F1
Drury Primary School
MOLD/BUCK CH7 ....43 G2
Dunkirk Trading Estate
CH/BCN CH1 ....11 G1
Eaton Golf Club
CHSE CH3 ....51 H2
Eaton Hotel
CH/BCN CH1 ....3 G3
Eccleston CE Primary School
CHSE CH3 ....49 E5
Elfed High School
MOLD/BUCK CH7 ....42 C2
Ewloe Castle
CQ CH5 ....31 E1
Ewloe Green Primary School
CQ CH5 ....31 F3
Expressway Business Park
CQ CH5 ....20 D3

The Firs School
CHNE CH2 ....25 F4
Flint Castle
FLINT CH6 ....5 E1
Flint Child Health Clinic
FLINT CH6 ....5 E3
Flint Community Hospital
FLINT CH6 ....4 D3
Flint FC
FLINT CH6 ....5 E2
Flint Golf Club
FLINT CH6 ....4 A4
Flint High School
FLINT CH6 ....4 D5
Flint Leisure Centre
FLINT CH6 ....4 D2
Flintshire Retail Park
FLINT CH6 ....4 D2
The Forum Shopping Centre
CH/BCN CH1 ....2 D4
Garden City Industrial Estate
CQ CH5 ....21 E1
Garden Lane Medical Centre
CH/BCN CH1 ....2 C2
Gateway Theatre
CH/BCN CH1 ....2 C4
The Gateway to Wales Hotel
CQ CH5 ....21 E2
General Cemetery
CHSW/BR CH4 ....36 D5
Glanrafon Primary School
MOLD/BUCK CH7 ....40 C4
Goffryn CP School
CQ CH5 ....19 E1
Greater Grace School
CHNE CH2 ....12 C2
Greyhound Retail Park
CH/BCN CH1 ....36 A1
Grosvenor Museum
CH/BCN CH1 ....2 E6
Grosvenor Nuffield Hospital
CHSW/BR CH4 ....48 D1
Grosvenor Shopping Centre
CH/BCN CH1 ....2 E5
Guilden Sutton Primary School
CHSE CH3 ....26 D4
Gwynedd Primary School
FLINT CH6 ....4 D4
Hammond School
CHNE CH2 ....26 B2
Handbridge Medical Centre
CHSW/BR CH4 ....2 E7
Happy Feet Health Centre
CQ CH5 ....19 H2
Hawarden Airport
CHSW/BR CH4 ....34 A5
Hawarden Castle
CQ CH5 ....32 D5
Hawarden Golf Club
CQ CH5 ....32 A4
Hawarden Health Centre
CQ CH5 ....32 C4
Hawarden Industrial Park
CHSW/BR CH4 ....33 G5
Hawarden Infant School
CQ CH5 ....32 C4
Heath Lane Medical Centre
CHSE CH3 ....37 H3
Heritage Centre
CH/BCN CH1 ....2 E5
Highfield Primary School
CH/BCN CH1 ....24 A5
Holiday Inn
CQ CH5 ....48 B5
Hoole CE Primary School
CHNE CH2 ....37 H1
Hoole Hall Hotel
CHSE CH3 ....26 B3
Huntington Primary School
CHSE CH3 ....49 H2
Innkeeper's Lodge Hotel
CHNE CH2 ....26 B3
CHSE CH3 ....38 C4
J H Godwin Primary School
CH/BCN CH1 ....23 G5
John Summers High School
CQ CH5 ....20 B4
King Charles Tower
CH/BCN CH1 ....2 E5
The Kings School
CHSW/BR CH4 ....48 C3
Kingsway High School
CHNE CH2 ....25 G4
Kus Industrial Estate
CQ CH5 ....45 F1
Lache Health Centre
CHSW/BR CH4 ....48 B2
Lache Primary School
CHSW/BR CH4 ....48 B2
Lakeside Business Village
CQ CH5 ....31 G3
Little Mountain Industrial
Estate *MOLD/BUCK* CH7 ...43 F3
The Little Theatre
CH/BCN CH1 ....2 E2
Mancot Clinic

Manor Lane Industrial Estate
CQ CH5 ....32 C2
CHSW/BR CH4 ....45 G1
Marches Medical Centre
MOLD/BUCK CH7 ....42 C2
Megabowl
CH/BCN CH1 ....36 A1
Merton House School
CHNE CH2 ....24 D5
Mickle Trafford Village School
CHNE CH2 ....26 D1
Mill Hotel
CH/BCN CH1 ....3 G3
Mill View Primary School
CHNE CH2 ....25 F3
Mold Business Park
MOLD/BUCK CH7 ....40 B5
Mold CC
MOLD/BUCK CH7 ....40 D2
Mold Child Health Clinic
MOLD/BUCK CH7 ....40 C2
Mold Community Hospital
MOLD/BUCK CH7 ....40 B2
Mold RFC
MOLD/BUCK CH7 ....40 D2
Mold Sports Centre
MOLD/BUCK CH7 ....40 C4
Mollington Banastre Hotel
CH/BCN CH1 ....24 A2
Mountain Lane Primary School
MOLD/BUCK CH7 ....42 D2
Mynydd Isa Junior School
MOLD/BUCK CH7 ....41 G1
New Gate
CH/BCN CH1 ....3 F5
Newton Primary School
CHNE CH2 ....25 F5
Northgate
CH/BCN CH1 ....2 D3
Northgate Arena Leisure
Centre *CHNE* CH2 ....2 D4
Northgate Medical Centre
CH/BCN CH1 ....2 D2
Northop Country Park Golf
Club *MOLD/BUCK* CH7 .....17 E5
Northop Hall Country House
Hotel *MOLD/BUCK* CH7 ...30 C1
Northop Hall Primary School
MOLD/BUCK CH7 ....18 A5
North Wales Health Authority
MOLD/BUCK CH7 ....46 B3
Odeon Theatre
CH/BCN CH1 ....2 D5
Oldfield County Primary
School *CHSE* CH3 ....38 B1
The Osteopathic Health
Centre *CH/BCN* CH1 ....36 C1
Outreach Theatre
MOLD/BUCK CH7 ....40 C3
Owl Halt Industrial Estate
CQ CH5 ....21 E5
Park Medical Centre
CHNE CH2 ....25 G5
Parkway Business Centre
CQ CH5 ....8 D4
Penarlag Primary School
CQ CH5 ....31 H2
Pentre Industrial Estate
CQ CH5 ....21 E5
Pentrobin St John the Baptist
VA School *CHSW/BR* CH4 ...44 A5
Pinfold Lane Industrial Estate
MOLD/BUCK CH7 ....30 B5
Premier Lodge
CHNE CH2 ....24 D4
The Queen Hotel
CH/BCN CH1 ....3 H2
Queensferry Industrial Estate
CQ CH5 ....20 D5
Queensferry Primary School
CQ CH5 ....20 B4
Queens Park High School
CHSW/BR CH4 ....48 C2
The Queens School
CH/BCN CH1 ....2 C4
Rector Drew Junior Aided
School *CQ* CH5 ....32 C4
The Ridings Infant School
CQ CH5 ....11 E5
Rowing Club
CQ CH5 ....3 G5
Rowton Hall Country House
Hotel *CHSE* CH3 ....50 D2
St Anthonys RC Primary
School *CHSW/BR* CH4 ......47 H1
St Clares RC Primary School
CHSE CH3 ....48 B2
St Davids High School
CHSW/BR CH4 ....35 F5
St Davids RC Primary School
MOLD/BUCK CH7 ....40 D2
St Davids Trading Estate
CHSW/BR CH4 ....35 G5
St Ethelwolds Primary School
CQ CH5 ....20 A5
St Martins Clinic

CQ CH5 ....32 C2
St Martins Gate
CH/BCN CH1 ....
St Mary's Centre
CH/BCN CH1 ....
St Marys RC Primary School
FLINT CH6 ....
St Oswalds CE Aided Primary
School *CH/BCN* CH1 ....
St Richard Gwyn RC High
School *FLINT* CH6 ....
St Theresas Primary School
CH/BCN CH1 ....
St Thomas of Canterbury
CE Jun Sch *CH/BCN* CH1 ...
St Werburghs & Columbas
RC Prim Sch *CHNE* CH2 ...
Saltney Clinic
CHSW/BR CH4 ....
Saltney Ferry Primary School
CHSW/BR CH4 ....
Sandycroft Industrial Estate
CQ CH5 ....
Sandycroft Primary School
CQ CH5 ....
Sealand Child Health Centre
CQ CH5 ....
Sealand Industrial Estate
CH/BCN CH1 ....
Sealand Primary School
CQ CH5 ....
Shotton Infant School
CQ CH5 ....
Soughton Hall Hotel
MOLD/BUCK CH7 ....
South Down Primary School
MOLD/BUCK CH7 ....
Spencer Industrial Estate
MOLD/BUCK CH7 ....
Sychdyn Primary School
MOLD/BUCK CH7 ....
Taliesin Junior School
MOLD/BUCK CH7 ....
Tarvin Road Medical Centre
CHSE CH3 ....
Thomas Wedge Junior School
CH/BCN CH1 ....
Town Hall & Mayors Parlour
CH/BCN CH1 ....
Travelodge
MOLD/BUCK CH7 ....
Upton by Chester High School
CHNE CH2 ....
Upton Heath CE Primary
School *CHNE* CH2 ....
Upton Westlea Primary
School *CHNE* CH2 ....
Venerable Edward Morgan
RC Primary School *CQ* CH5 ...
Vicars Cross Golf Club
CHSE CH3 ....
Victoria Infant School
CH/BCN CH1 ....
Virgin Cinemas
CH/BCN CH1 ....
Watergate
CH/BCN CH1 ....
Wats Dyke Infant School
MOLD/BUCK CH7 ....
Waverton Community
Primary School *CHSE* CH3 ...
Welsh College of Horticulture
MOLD/BUCK CH7 ....
Wepre Park
CQ CH5 ....
Wepre Primary School
CQ CH5 ....
West Cheshire College
CHSW/BR CH4 ....
Western Avenue Medical
Centre *CH/BCN* CH1 ....
Westminster Hotel
CH/BCN CH1 ....
Westwood Primary School
MOLD/BUCK CH7 ....
Woodfield Primary School
CHNE CH2 ....
Wood Memorial CP School
CHSW/BR CH4 ....
Ysgol Belmont
MOLD/BUCK CH7 ....
Ysgol Croes Atti Primary
School *FLINT* CH6 ....
Ysgol Delyn
MOLD/BUCK CH7 ....
Ysgol Maes Garmon
MOLD/BUCK CH7 ....
Ysgol Owen Jones
MOLD/BUCK CH7 ....

Acknowledgements

The Post Office is a registered trademark of Post Office Ltd. in the UK and other countries.

Schools address data provided by Education Direct.

Petrol station information supplied by Johnsons

One-way street data provided by © Tele Atlas N.V. Tele Atlas

The statement on the front cover of this atlas is sourced, selected and quoted
from a reader comment and feedback form received in 2004

Garden centre information provide
Garden Centre Association Britains best garden cen
Wyevale Garden Cen

AA **Street by Street** QUESTIONNAIRE

Dear Atlas User
Your comments, opinions and recommendations are very important to us.
So please help us to improve our street atlases by taking a few minutes
to complete this simple questionnaire.

You do not need a stamp (unless posted outside the UK). If you do not want to remove this page from your street atlas, then photocopy it or write your answers on a plain sheet of paper.

Send to: The Editor, AA Street by Street, FREEPOST SCE 4598,
Basingstoke RG21 4GY

ABOUT THE ATLAS...

Which city/town/county did you buy?

Are there any features of the atlas or mapping that you find particularly useful?

Is there anything we could have done better?

Why did you choose an AA Street by Street atlas?

Did it meet your expectations?

Exceeded ☐ **Met all** ☐ **Met most** ☐ **Fell below** ☐

Please give your reasons

Where did you buy it?

For what purpose? (please tick all applicable)

To use in your own local area ☐   To use on business or at work ☐

Visiting a strange place ☐   In the car ☐   On foot ☐

Other (please state)

LOCAL KNOWLEDGE...

Local knowledge is invaluable. Whilst every attempt has been made to make the information contained in this atlas as accurate as possible, should you notice any inaccuracies, please detail them below (if necessary, use a blank piece of paper) or e-mail us at *streetbystreet@theAA.com*

ABOUT YOU...

Name (Mr/Mrs/Ms)

Address

Postcode

Daytime tel no

E-mail address

Which age group are you in?

Under 25 ☐   25-34 ☐   35-44 ☐   45-54 ☐   55-64 ☐   65+ ☐

Are you an AA member?   YES ☐   NO ☐

Do you have Internet access?   YES ☐   NO ☐

Thank you for taking the time to complete this questionnaire. Please send it to us as soon as possible, and remember, you do not need a stamp (unless posted outside the UK).

ML081z